An Ohio State Man:
Esco Sarkkinen
Remembers OSU Football

Esco Sarkkinen in 1937

Esco Sarkkinen as an OSU coach

William Harper
Go Bucks!
2006

An Ohio
State Man

by William L. Harper

Enthea Press
Atlanta — Columbus

AN OHIO STATE MAN
Esco Sarkkinen Remembers OSU Football

ISBN 0-89804-850-8

Contents

Esco practicing in Ohio Stadium

An Ohio State Man

Coach Alert!

Coach Esco Sarkkinen drifted over to our table with mischief in his eyes. "Since you guys know all about Buckeye football, can you name the five football traditions at Ohio State?"

My friends, Ron and Doug, and I began identifying the traditions—but much too slowly for Coach. Feigning impatience, he ticked them off:

- The tuba player dotting the 'i' in Script Ohio.
- The Captains Breakfast.
- The Senior Tackle.
- Gold Pants (a charm) for beating Michigan.
- A buckeye tree for each Ohio State All-American, planted near Ohio Stadium.

Coach smiled a moment, then sat down to join us.

Weekday mornings were charged with football reminiscences when my friends and I gathered to start the day at Mill Street Bagels. During the time we met for coffee and conversation, Coach Sarkkinen usually stopped by to pick up his favorite sandwich for lunch.

While waiting for his carryout order to be filled, Coach would order coffee and raid the tray of bagel samples on the counter. Sometimes, he circulated among the customers or paused to chat with staff. Other times, he would sit down and linger at our table or those nearby. These were the moments we all hoped for—because they signaled another discussion of Buckeye football.

Aside from fresh bagels and sumptuous cinnamon rolls, Coach was the main attraction at Mill Street. When the counter staff spotted him approaching the bagel shop, they called out "Coach Alert! Coach Alert!" and began preparing for his arrival. An air of expectancy permeated the shop.

Coach's popularity was evidenced by a photo enlargement from his playing days, conspicuously posted on the shop's main cash register, emblazoned with these words:

"MILL STREET'S FAVORITE CUSTOMER"

Coach Sarkkinen was renowned for his Ohio State trivia and gridiron stories, the foundation of his friendly repartee with others. He often used his storehouse of recollections in an easy, natural way to begin conversations and break the ice. For instance, when Esco joined our table one morning, my friends and I were put to a test with this series of questions:

"How are all the Ohio State experts this morning?"

The three of us mumbled incoherently.

"You all know the main campus, right?"

We nodded affirmatively.

"Familiar with everything, right?"

We were not so sure of that.

"Well then, which one of you can tell me where I can find Lake Hayes?"

Coach leaned back in his chair while enjoying our puzzled musings on the location of Lake Hayes. Then he arose and went to the counter to claim his carryout order. After returning and taking a seat, he continued the exchange.

"O.K., who's got the answer?"

"Is Lake Hayes a nickname for Mirror Lake?"

"No-o."

"Could it be the Olentangy River?"

"No-o-o."

"How about one of the ponds on campus?"

"No-o-o-o."

Pretending exasperation, Coach finally asked: "Give up?"

"Yes, yes, yes," from his admirers.

After pausing for dramatic effect, his answer came: "Lake Hayes is the practice field!"

Given this curious answer, we were certain Coach's explanation would be intriguing.

"Coach Hayes was serious about getting the Buckeyes ready to play football in bad weather and in the Big Ten this meant playing in mud. So, periodically, he would get the ground crew to drag out hoses and soak the practice field until it was as muddy as could be. He often overdid the sprinkling and water flooded the turf.

"Because of the soaked turf and standing water, we coaches dubbed the practice field 'Lake Hayes.' At times it got so bad that we had to get two pairs of shoes, one pair for practice while the other pair was drying!"

Ron, who knew I was working on another book, turned to me one day and said: "You know, Bill, if someone doesn't write down Esco's stories, they'll be lost—why don't you take some time and do it?"

Doug chimed in: "That's right, Buckeye fans everywhere would love to read Sark's stories."

Thus the idea for this tribute to Coach Sarkkinen was born.

Esco with Bill Harper at Mill Street Bagels

Notes to Himself

Sark was a thoughtful man who loved life, engaging it through literature, philosophy, history, warfare, sports, family, comedy, and current events. As he came across a saying he admired—or was inspired by one of his own—he would jot it down. He left behind little notes filled with hundreds of sayings. I have picked some of the ones I think shed the most light on Esco Sarkkinen the man and have scattered them throughout the text. Here are some samples:

"I live my life, and let everyone else live theirs." —*Esco Sarkkinen.*

"Sleep with a dog, and you will wake up with fleas."—*Socrates.*

"Keep the faith and a warm heart."—*H.L. Mencken.*

"The Truth is rarely pure and is seldom simple."—*Oscar Wilde.*

"The older I get, the more I remember things that never happened."—*Mark Twain.*

O-H-I-O

Prayer works best when your players are big and talented. —Knute Rockne

Esko [Esco] Sarkkinen was born in Conneaut, Ohio in 1918 and attended Harding High School, located in nearby Fairport Harbor. He was an outstanding athlete, lettering in basketball, track, and football. He gained quite a reputation and was eagerly sought after by several Ohio schools.

Esco displayed his tongue-in-cheek humor on a senior page in his high school annual, the *Harbor Light*. Despite his well-known commitment to playing college football, he states that his ambition is "to sell Hart, Schaffner & Marx suits to Mahatma Gandhi."

After graduating from Harding High, Esco entered Ohio State University in the fall of 1936. With around 200 other OSU freshmen, Esco answered the call for first-year football players. Starting at left end, his talent began to show—he was one of thirty-nine players to earn their freshman sweaters and numerals. As a sophomore in 1937, he earned his first varsity letter. Other letters were awarded in 1938 and 1939, his junior and senior seasons.

"When I played at OSU," Sark recalled, "there were three varsity letters. The first letter, usually awarded as a sophomore, was a gray Block O, worn above the left pocket on a scarlet cardigan sweater. The second was a similar gray Block O centered on the front of a scarlet pullover sweater, awarded in the junior year. The senior letter was a gray Block O on a scarlet blanket, and is still being used today."

Playing much larger than his 6'1" frame and 195 pounds would suggest, Esco's teammates called him "Big Sark." The nickname stuck in part and he would later become just "Sark" to his friends and coaching colleagues.

Big Sark had a younger brother, Eino, whose career as an OSU halfback overlapped his own. Eino, being shorter and lighter, appeared as "Little Sark" in the local press but his real nickname was "Shorty."

The presence of two, fair, Finnish brothers on the OSU varsity provided an irresistible, human interest slant on Buckeye football. Big Sark and Little Sark—the "brother act" from Fairport Harbor—were a hit with sports writers and fans.

By the way, these Finnish names are pronounced:

Esco (ess´- co)
Eino (eee´- no)
Sarkkinen (sark´- kuh - nen)

Esco earned a starting berth at end as a sophomore but missed the opening game due to a groin injury—minor injuries would continue to hamper him in all but his senior year. Even so, as a junior in 1938, he made second-team Big Ten All-Star and received a meritorious award from the

Esco wearing his sophomore letter sweater

All-American board of football. Sark became an "official" All-American when Grantland Rice, with board consultation, named him to the 1939 Collier's All-American team. Consensus came with selection to six of eight All-American teams named by the national press services and major newspapers. After becoming an All-American, Big Sark appeared in the numerous all-star games, including the Blue-Gray classic.

Popularity was Esco's due. Large and small newspapers in Ohio and the Midwest reported his football exploits, awards, travel, education and social activities, often with large-spread features and photographs. A testimonial dinner for him drew about 400 family and friends to the Suomi Finnish Church Hall in Fairport Harbor.

Esco was selected for membership in Bucket and Dipper, and to Sphinx, at Ohio State. He was honored by the Big Ten as OSU's top athlete-scholar. He played hard, he studied hard, and he put himself through college. One summer, Sark worked in a chemical factory. During others, he worked on an ore freighter plying the Great Lakes, shipping out as second cook.

Symbol of an outstanding college career

Acknowledged as a BMOC—big man on campus—Esco was a sought-after source of opinion on the campus scene. Radio commentators and press reporters, eager to capitalize on his star quality, could count on a ready quip to entertain their listeners and readers. For instance, when asked about the key to his academic success, he replied: "Stay away from fickle femininity until the weekends—but have a four or five-day weekend if you wish."

Described as the "big blond Ohio State end"—and he was handsome with his tousled fair hair and winsome smile—Sark was often profiled in print for his scholarship, admiration of past Buckeye greats, and interest in OSU grid lore.

At the conclusion of his senior season, Esco publicly announced his intention to become a football coach. Public speculation on a professional football career ceased when he spurned an an offer to join the Green Bay Packers.

After graduation, Esco began his coaching career in 1940 as the assistant coach under Coach E. J. Wilson at the Lancaster (Ohio) High School. When Wilson retired, Esco assumed the position of head coach. After two opening losses in 1941, the Golden Gales reeled off seven consecutive victories for their first league championship since 1933. For meritorious service to youngsters, a Lancaster citizen committee voted Sark "man of the year"—at the age of twenty-three!

Was Big Sark great? You bet, according to his position coach, Sid Gillman, who himself had been a starring flanker.

"Sark does it all.

"He's a great blocker, hitting hard and clean; he is a near perfect pass catcher and can make yards after a reception; he's always in a position to help the runner downfield. On the defense, Sark piles up the interference if he doesn't make the tackle himself. No team this year has been able to run around him with any degree of success. He's a smashing tackler, loving that hard contact and judging his man with deadly accuracy. He's so fast, running the 100 in 10 seconds, that no halfbacks have been able to speed past him; his coverage of punts has always been a strong point.

"He's just the kind of player who senses where trouble may be, and makes sure to be there…"

Big Sark made All-America while at a considerable disadvantage—it was the policy at OSU to emphasize and promote team achievements, not those of individual players. Paul Hornung, a local sportswriter, wrote a stinging condemnation of this policy under this headline "Bucks Must Earn All-America Minus 'Drumming.' He opened a lengthy article with this salvo:

"Special note to editors: Don't hold your Sark-kinen-Scott All-American campaigns until Ohio State's publicity department gives a downbeat. You'll still be waiting in 1950…"

So, without any official 'drumming,' Sark made All-America on his own abilities and the support of coaches and the press, winning out over many other talented, well-promoted candidates.

Having flattened the Cornell end, Esco
takes out the blocking back

Seconds later, he tackles the ball carrier.
Photos are from the 1939 game film.

"When I played at Ohio State," Sark recalled, "the Old Man—Head Coach Francis Schmidt—had an offensive system with nearly three hundred plays, five to six times as many as his rivals. He zealously guarded his offensive plays, almost to the point of paranoia. Under lock and key in the physical education building (later named Larkins Hall), access to the master play collection was limited to Coach Schmidt and his coaching staff.

"The play books given to Buckeye players were sparse and coded. In my end book, for example, a page would give the number of the play and just a few Xs and Os on the action I was to take. As a consequence, it was impossible for me to compile information on the OSU offense from my own play book.

"After finishing my last season, I got a coaching job at Lancaster High, not far from Columbus, but after three years under Coach Schmidt, I had no offensive system to take with me. I took my dilemma to Sid Gillman, my former end coach, and we schemed together on how to get the of-

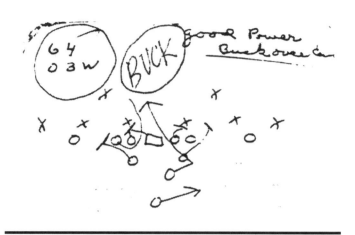

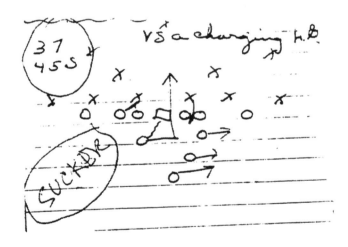

Two plays from Esco's play book.
Top diagrams a buck over center.
Bottom diagrams a play to sucker the defense.

fensive system needed for my new job. Sid came up with the solution.

" 'The Old Man goes to lunch every day between twelve and two o'clock. Come around Monday during that time and I'll get the master plays from his office for you to copy.'

"At the beginning of the week, Sid and I went to work but made little progress during long lunches—it took more than a week to copy the plays I needed. Although there were many anxious moments, I finally had an offensive system ready for my new job.

"I often chuckle at Sid's daring complicity during our lunch time raids. A dusty copy of Coach Schmidt's offense is stored in my attic, now more than fifty years old."

From Coach Schmidt's large inventory of plays, Esco copied about one hundred to take with him to Lancaster High, those that could be run with schoolboy talent. These plays he inked into a small notebook, tattered from considerable use.

Many of the plays in his playbook are mere sketches, obviously done hurriedly, but still catching the essential features of each play. Like Francis Schmidt's "razzle-dazzle" offense under which he had played, Esco installed a multiple offense at Lancaster High, using four basic formations—quite inventive for the early 1940's!

"When I was the end coach at Ohio State," remarked Sid Gillman, former general manager and head coach of the San Diego Chargers, "I was fortunate enough to have two tremendous ends. One was Esco Sarkkinen and the other Merle Wendt—neither of these two players got

Esco catches pass from quarterback Don Scott

the attention they deserved. Although Esco did make All-American in 1939, he never received the full accolades he merited as a player.

"Esco was a great end. He had good size, good speed and hands that wouldn't quit. Head Coach Schmidt and I just loved him. He was a real smart football player—very bright.

"Esco's coaching potential was exceptional. He had everything needed to become a top head coach. For a coach like myself, who had a driving need to keep moving up in the coaching ranks, it is extremely difficult for me to understand how Esco—or any coach—could be satisfied with assistant coaching as a career.

"But Esco was very satisfied to be an assistant coach at Ohio State. He loved the university and its football program, and was content to contribute his coaching talent to them. The Buckeyes benefited greatly from an excellent coach who found great satisfaction in recruiting, evaluating and schooling football talent. In every way, Esco Sarkkinen was an Ohio State Man!"

Teaming Up

*Love is a furnace, but it will not cook the
stew.*   *—Spanish proverb*

After he graduated from OSU in 1940, Esco
Sarkkinen married Freda Jane Burkhardt in
Cleveland's Old Stone Church, attended by a small
party of family and friends. Freda, a former home-
coming queen candidate, had graduated from
Ohio State a year earlier than Esco. Their mar-
riage was squeezed in between two football commitments.

"Esco played in a college All-Star Game against
the Green Bay Packers on Thursday, August 29,
flew to Cleveland on Friday, and married Freda
on Saturday," said Esco's daughter, Sandy. "Due
to plans for a short wedding trip, Esco turned
down an invitation to participate in a college all-
star game with the Cleveland Rams on the upcoming Wednesday.

"However, because Esco was a regional sports
figure with drawing power, the game's sponsor

was determined to have him play in the Cleveland game. Esco negotiated a deal—he would play in the all-star game if the sponsor would pick up the couple's expenses for their honeymoon. Freda approved and Esco showed up for the all-star game.

"Ever the clever negotiator, Esco enjoyed a pleasant week with his bride at the Hotel Cleveland while his all-star teammates camped out in training quarters at John Carroll University.

"Freda quickly learned what it meant to be a

Freda, Sandy, and Esco Sarkkinen

coach's wife, but without surprise. Before getting married, she and Esco had frankly discussed all the implications of a coaching career—long hours, stress, and the possibility of moving ten to twelve times for steady employment. Freda and Esco started off as a coaching 'team' with their eyes wide open."

Sandra Sue Hayes is the married name of Sark's daughter, Sandy. Because of the lengthy association between her father and Woody Hayes, the first question that invariably comes up is:

"Are you related to Woody Hayes?"

And the answer is: "No, I am not."

Sandy is happily married to a police officer named Chris Hayes. She maintains long-standing Buckeye ties through tailgating, football games, and other sports-related events at OSU. Fun loving as she is, Sandy is slow to reveal her true identity—there simply is too much humorous advantage in the misperceptions of others.

War Years

Honor, Duty, Country—West Point motto

While Esco was at Ohio State, the widespread military aggression leading up to World War II had already begun. It was only a matter of time until the United States would be drawn into global conflict.

During the 1930's, the Soviet Union cast a threatening shadow over Finland, the Sarkkinen homeland. Finnish populations and culture inside Russia were repressed and many Finns fled homeward to escape a totalitarian regime. When demands for military base concessions were refused, the Russians launched a military attack in November, 1939, but were repulsed by Finland in the Winter War of 1939-40.

On campus, Esco and Eino involved themselves in war relief efforts for the Finnish Aid Committee. For instance, during the half-time of a 1939 Ohio State-Illinois basketball game, Eino made several passionate appeals, speaking in Finnish.

Esco, also a featured speaker, served as translator. When Eino launched into his final appeal, he grew more excitable and raised his fist menacingly. Esco told the crowd it wouldn't be wise to translate his brother's tirade because Eino "was talking about Josef Stalin."

"Esco Sarkkinen, who sings Finnish lullabies to his fraternity brothers, says that the Finns aren't worried about fighting the Russians, they are just wondering where to find ground enough to bury all of them."—*Press clipping, in 1939.*

After two seasons at Lancaster High, Esco enlisted in the Coast Guard and attended its Officer Candidate School at Manhattan Beach. Freda, awaiting their first child, lived nearby on Staten Island. After graduating as a "90-day wonder" with the rank of Lieutenant J.G., Sark was assigned to the New London Coast Guard

Station in Connecticut. After Esco and Freda took up residence on station, their daughter Sandy was born in October, 1942. Esco played end for the New London Coast Guard team and later became its line coach.

"Enlisting in the Coast Guard provides a clue to my father's character," Sandy confided: "Esco was always a cautious person and not a big risk taker. This caution, I believe, was reflected in his choice of military service. Curious as it may seem for the coach of a contact sport, Esco was a gentle person and somewhat of a pacifist. Even so, as the son of immigrant parents, he deeply appreciated living in America. His decision to serve in the Coast Guard was, I believe, a way of being true to his character while providing honorable service to his country."

Esco's brother, Eino, left Ohio State before graduation and entered the military, as would many athletes during World War II. He enlisted in the Army Air Corps and received his aviator wings in October, 1941, shortly before Esco entered the Coast Guard Academy.

The names Esco and Eino were always a source of confusion, because both brothers had lettered in football at Ohio State. Even though Eino regularly played halfback, he had at one time practiced at end when Sark was injured.

To boost morale, the Army scheduled football games between an Army all-star team and three professional teams during the 1942 season—the New York Giants, the Brooklyn Dodgers, and the Chicago Bears.

All three games were scheduled to be played within a nine-day span. Robert Neyland, head football coach at Tennessee, had already been recalled to Army service and was assigned the job of organizing and coaching the Army All-Stars.

When Coach Neyland scheduled tryouts at Yale, where the All-Stars would practice for five weeks, Eino signed in as "E. Sarkkinen, from Ohio State."

Of course, Neyland immediately recognized the name "E. Sarkkinen" and thought he was getting an All-American end. Without asking Eino what position he played, Coach Neyland put him on the left flank and called for a button-hook pass, explaining the route he wanted run. The ball was snapped, Eino ran an excellent route, hooked back, and made a superb catch. Neyland was exceptionally well-pleased and exclaimed with enthusiasm: "Well, boys, that's how an All-American does it!"

Esco had driven from New London to New Haven to observe the tryouts. Standing behind the fence surrounding the practice field, he was beside himself with laughter at his brother's chicanery.

Eino successfully posed as Esco during the All-Stars' practice period, but when it came to facing the pros, he was outclassed playing end. Coach Neyland, of course, was disappointed. When Eino was ready to return to his outfit, Coach Neyland sent him on his way with this remark:

"Your play has been disappointing, Esco, and I'm left wondering how you ever made All-American!"

Homecoming

Nothing comes closer to a religious experience than America's fervor for football.   —Knute Rockne

Ohio State was known as "The Graveyard of Coaches," due to the rapid turnover of head coaches in the 1940's. Francis Schmidt left as the decade began. Paul Brown departed not long after a national championship season. Carroll Widdoes lasted two seasons, Paul Bixler one, and Wes Fesler four. All had produced winning programs.

In this volatile decade, Esco Sarkkinen began his college coaching career in 1946 as an assistant football coach under Paul Bixler. When Bixler left, Sark was retained by Wes Fesler and remained with him through the 1950 season.

Everyone breathed a sigh of relief when the highly-regarded Missouri head coach, Don Faurot, became the new head coach of the Buckeyes in 1951. But, upon returning home with the job in hand and reconsidering the pressure that came with it, Faurot decided to stay at Missouri. Re-opening the search for a head coach proved embarrassing and controversial. Wayne Woodrow Hayes interviewed successfully, was appointed, and began preparation for the 1951 season.

"When Woody Hayes was hired," recalled Sandy, "Esco was not optimistic. Because of Woody's emotional coaching style, Esco did not expect Coach Hayes to last more than three or four years. But, after getting organized, Woody began winning—and the rest is history."

Esco stayed on as an assistant coach under Woody Hayes—and remained with him until retirement, capping a 32-year coaching career at Ohio State.

Loyalty

If a man has one friend, he is rich.—Sark

"Did you ever try to hire Esco as an assistant coach after you took the head coaching job at Michigan?" Bo Schembechler was once asked.

"You know," he replied with a chuckle, "Sark was so committed to Ohio State that the idea of offering him a job at Michigan never even occurred to me!"

"Loyalty was important to Coach Hayes," emphasized Esco. "He believed loyalty was a two-way street. As long as his players and coaches remained loyal to him, they could rely on his loyalty in return. We could make some awful mistakes at times and Woody could come down on us pretty hard. But we were always certain that when the chips were down we could count on his backing and support."

Gene Fekete, a former OSU assistant coach, agrees.

"At the initial staff meeting with our new head coach, I expected to talk football, but Woody opened with a half-hour discourse on loyalty. Right from the beginning, loyalty became a cornerstone of our Buckeye program. Woody's two-way approach to loyalty enabled him to capitalize upon the four experienced assistant coaches he retained from Wes Fesler's staff—Esco, Ernie Godfrey, Harry Strobel, and myself—all with Big Ten experience at a time when Woody had none."

"Coach Hayes didn't have to spend much time talking about loyalty—everyone knew where he stood," according to Jim Houston, former Buckeye and two-time All-American end. "Loyalty was an honorable, unquestionable principle. Woody talked about loyalty broadly, in terms of the team, the students, the alumni, and the University."

40

One morning, when Sark and I were reminiscing about his long coaching career at OSU, I asked:

"How come you stayed at Ohio State for thirty-two years, Coach? Surely, you must have had opportunities to coach elsewhere."

"Yes, it's true that I had lots of offers to move on, but once I got the Ohio State job, with all the tradition and great players and great coaches and great fans, nothing else appealed to me."

Coaching

The Swedes call it "Is i mage!" —Ice in the belly! —Sark

"In my mind," Coach Sarkkinen began, "there are six types of coaches.

"First is the Blackboard Coach with his Xs and Os and a genius for the game—the innovator.

"Second is the Game Coach, the field general who can organize a coaching staff, a team, and an annual campaign.

"Third is the Practice Coach who teaches, drills and disciplines his players daily.

"Fourth is the Recruiting Coach who identifies outstanding athletes and cultivates positive relationships with them.

"Fifth is the Scouting Coach who gathers and analyzes information on opposing teams.

"Sixth is the Fund Raising Coach who plays an extremely important role in today's athletic environment.

"Playing football at the highest level is like

going to war every weekend. And when you go into battle, you want a general—a game coach—who stands above the fray, confident in his plans and troops, able to make decisions rapidly with ice in his veins, the man who never gets rattled and retains control of the game. This type of coach develops a strategy, or plan, before the game and devises tactics accordingly, but has the ability to make keen tactical changes on the move.

"Some of the game coaches that come to mind who can remain aloof in this way, while still intensely involved in a game, are Bear Bryant, John McKay, Marv Levy and Joe Paterno. Other successful head coaches have this quality too, but not to the same degree.

"Among the coaches I have known, I believe Sid Gillman is the best blackboard coach in the game. He is an astute student of football and an inventive genius. He claims to be retired, but if I call his home in Carlsbad, I'll bet on hearing a VCR or film projector whirring away in the background on a consulting assignment.

"Sid is completely absorbed in the technical

side of football. Although I have known him more than fifty years, relatively few social words have passed between us. A blackboard coach like Sid puts invention and tactical surprise in the hands of the game coach and inspires the other members of his coaching staff.

"There are many good practice coaches, usually unheralded. If game coaches may be likened to generals, practice coaches are his staff who carry out the key tasks he assigns, such as preparing an annual campaign, getting ready for weekly encounters, teaching and training players under them.

"Almost all coaches recruit as part of their duties, usually within a geographic area of the country or in a regional hotbed of talent where they have connections. The recruiting coach paves the way for the head coach who has the final say on offering a scholarship. In the past few years, the Buckeyes have just been a recruit or two away from perfect seasons, so tremendous emphasis is now put on recruiting.

"The head coach is usually the game coach but also plays a much larger university role today as the fund raising coach. He serves both the academic and athletic programs, and usually is a strong link to the alumni, business community, individuals, charitable causes, and media."

"Coaching is an exclusive profession," confided Sark. "What we talk about when coaches get together is very different than what we discuss with outsiders. You have to realize that coaching is a high risk profession because of the emphasis on winning. Of course, not all teams can have winning seasons."

"I'm rather proud of the racial progress in my profession and college athletics in general," Esco said once.

"There was a time when college football was an all-white affair. But coaches like Bear Bryant, and other coaches too, began recruiting players on the basis of talent not skin color. The important thing is that he and others like him won!

"Winning was important in changing attitudes.

"This was true in the pro ranks too. Throughout most of my career there was a lot of coaching prejudice based on race, religion, and enthnicity. I think Vince Lombardi, at Green Bay, broke the ice permanently. After he won five NFL titles in the 1960's, no one cared any more about his Italian name, or the names of many other fine coaches.

"Just take a look at the makeup of athletic teams today. There's lots of acceptance and cooperation—performance and winning are the measures. I think the record shows we're doing a lot better than the general population—helping to lead the way through media exposure."

Bear Bryant was talking to an alumni group in rural Alabama and was blunt as always. When questioned about taking Alabama to the top of collegiate football, he advised his Crimson Tide audience: "You folks have a choice to make. You can have a segregated team or you can have a national championship team—but you can't have both!"

"Esco Sarkkinen was one of the smartest coaches I have been associated with in my career," said Jim Stillwagon, "he certainly had been a great football player, an All-American, and this helped him get his points across to his position players. Sark was naturally fair-handed, a great people manager, and seemed to coach almost effortlessly—he was always upbeat and happy, every day. He was tops in terms of assessing talent and teams. Esco would have made a great pro coach," remarked Stillwagon, a two-time All-American who bypassed the NFL for stardom in the Canadian Football League.

"I played offensive end at Ohio State," said Jan White, "and usually practiced on another part of the field when Coach Sarkkinen was working with his defensive ends. Even from a distance he was impressive to watch.

"Sark coached in a positive way, inspiring his players. His coaching style was just the opposite of some fire-and-brimstone, frothing-at-the-mouth type coaches who rely on intimidation and brow-beating. He brought his own outstanding playing skills to coaching—he was a player's coach.

"It was marvelous to watch Sark's defensive ends give everything they had for him; they wanted to do well by him. He had the ability to get his players to play above their skill level—way over their heads. Sark fostered a camaraderie that led to close-knit relationships, bolstering team allegiance in the process.

"The longer I am away from my active playing days, the more I appreciate the coaching ability of Esco Sarkkinen," concluded White, a three-year letterman in 1968-70.

"I have always been impressed by the teaching ability and ingenuity of Sarkkinen. On many occasions, he has taken a man and played him the way he could play the best, rather than make him fit into a set pattern." —*Woody Hayes, 1978*

"Sark had one quality that everyone playing under him appreciated," recalled former player Tom Marendt. "Whenever you goofed up, he never corrected or criticized you in front of the other players. He would take you off to the side for privacy. Coach was not a wimp. He could be very demanding and wouldn't hesitate to get in your face—but never within earshot of your fellow team members. This considerate kind of one-on-one coaching was rare and all of us appreciated it."

"The key to Esco Sarkkinen's coaching," Jim Houston emphasized, "was infinite detail. The first thing Sark taught about playing defensive end was proper position: inside foot up, outside foot back, feet pointed toward the goal line, and shoulders parallel with the line of scrimmage.

"From this position, Sark drilled us to come off the ball with three precise steps and quickly assess our situation. We were schooled to take our cues from the initial movement of the play, particularly the actions of the offensive end and backs. Was it an inside play? A sweep? A reverse? An option? A reverse? Or a pass? After reading cues and checking for blocking ends and reverses—we were free to pursue the ball.

"On inside plays, for example, we resisted a driving shoulder block from the opposing end with an aggressive forearm shiver or arm lift—we were instructed to work through the blocker rather than go around him or play him off with our hands. On sweeps, we tried to hand fight to keep the blocker away from our legs, shedding him whenever possible. We gave ground grudgingly!

"On runs, we charged offensive blocking backs to catch them as quickly as possible, before they could develop power and momentum, keeping them away from our legs! On options, we would 'cat-n-mouse' the quarterback down the line to keep him, or a running back, from turning up field. On passes, as on all plays, we were taught to penetrate to the depth of the ball behind the line.

"A variety of individual techniques were used to carry out these general moves, and Sark was tops at adapting these to the talents of individual players. Overall, our defensive play was aggressive—we didn't just play wait-and-see football and let the offense come to us.

"These words on defensive end play only begin to scratch the surface of Sark's coaching. On offense, whether it was blocking or trapping or tackling, we were taught to do it precisely and consistently. We tried to do it Esco's way rather than our own. After all, he had been an All-American end and had been there—and we respected that. We paid attention when Esco was coaching.

"Esco's style of coaching contrasted sharply with that of Coach Hayes. Esco was everybody's friend and buddy—-we liked being around him and would do anything he asked. With Coach Hayes, however, you could only get personal after your Buckeye career was over. While you were a player, you did what Woody said because it was his way or the highway!"

"I don't believe there's a finer end coach in the country than Coach Esco Sarkkinen..."
— *Woody Hayes, in 1957*

Woody Hayes and Esco Sarkkinen confer

"Sark was much more than an end coach. He was very knowledgeable about all defensive and offensive aspects of the game," commented Pandel Savic, a former Buckeye quarterback. "At one point in my career, I was having trouble with my passing game—throwing behind my receivers, mostly. Sark came up with one his colorful rib-ticklers to help me:

" 'Throwing passes, Pandel, is just like duck hunting. Have you ever been duck hunting?'

" 'No, I haven't, Coach.'

" 'Well, in order to shoot ducks you have to aim in front of them—you have to aim where they will be instead of where they are. That way, when you pull the trigger, the duck and the shot will arrive at the same spot at the same time. That's how you shoot ducks.

" 'Throwing a pass is just like duck hunting. You have to throw the ball where you think the receiver will be so he and the ball can come together at the same spot at the same time. So, when you're passing, Pandel, think about shooting ducks.' "

"There was a solid bond between Woody Hayes and Esco Sarkkinen," according to Bill Mallory, former OSU assistant coach and retired head coach at Indiana. "Coach Hayes often asked, 'What do you think, Sark?' and was attentive when Sark replied. It was clear that Coach Hayes respected his thinking and good judgment. For newer members of the staff like myself, Sark was a steadying influence. He had already been coaching at OSU for twenty years when I arrived for the 1966 season and had been a member of Coach Hayes' staff from its inception."

"Sark had a great sense of knowing when it was time to do nothing," Earle Bruce recalled, "Coach Hayes was relentless in staff meetings— he would ask questions, expect immediate answers, and was impatient when he didn't get them. Moreover, if you came up with an answer that Woody didn't like, you could get into deep trouble.

"Sark had his own polite way of dealing with potentially explosive situations, through cigarette smoking. Whenever Woody asked him a question, Sark would slowly keep on puffing, pensively, as if conjuring up an answer. After a while, Coach Hayes would become impatient and move on. Gradually, the controversial situation would fizzle out without any harsh words being spoken.

"Sark had an effective diplomatic air about him that put him in good stead with Coach Hayes and all of us. He was the greatest assistant coach ever at Ohio State. Knowledgeable and hard working, he covered every detail. He was soft-spoken, humorous, and fun to be with, especially at lunch where he gave free rein to his gourmet instincts. Sark was one of the most positive individuals I have ever known."

"I was always amazed at the way Coach Hayes and Esco got along together. Woody, as you know," explained Bo Schembechler, "was a real emotional guy who could really get worked up over mistakes and shortcomings. I can still see him standing at the chalkboard, stabbing it with chalk, whacking it for emphasis. And while all of us were ready to run for cover, I would look over and see Sark just calmly sitting there—as if he almost enjoyed watching the explosive antics of our head coach."

"I played defensive end for Esco Sarkkinen in the spring of 1971, but switched positions afterward," explained Fred Pagac, now assistant head football coach at Ohio State. "Although he was no longer my position coach, we remained friends on the field and long after I graduated.

"In some ways, Sark and Woody were very similar.

"Both men had a great passion for the game of football, and could instill this passion in other coaches and players. My own passion for the game can be traced to both of them. Both men were also workaholics, though not in a negative sense; they truly enjoyed work and it was the central focus of their lives. My own work ethic was formed under them.

"But in many ways, Sark was his own man.

"Quick-witted and original, Sark was funny with a dry sense of humor. Whenever he was in a social situation sprinkled with Buckeye players, for instance, he would rate them No. 1 through No. 5 in terms of ability—as a joke. He even named me No. 1 several times, even though I was rubbing shoulders with some pretty talented guys.

"Among Sark's outstanding qualities were motivation and competitiveness. He truly understood people and could motivate them in a non-threatening way. He wanted to win and was willing to pay the price.

"The foundation of my approach to football comes from coaches like Woody and Sark—aggressive, hard-hitting, daring, and inventive."

"Ohio State is a school where there is keen competition for assistant coaching positions," Sark recalled.

"One day I had a call from Rick Forzano, a coach at the University of South Carolina. He told me South Carolina had a promising young coach who was ready to move up—that he wanted to coach at Ohio State so much that he would probably be willing to pay his own way. Forzano asked me to have Woody Hayes and the coaching staff consider his colleague for any openings.

"Because Harry Strobel was retiring, we had an opening for the '68 season. After evaluating lots of candidates, an assistant coaching position was offered to the young coach from South Carolina—and that's the story on how Lou Holtz came to be an assistant coach at Ohio State."

The career of Lou Holtz, who for eleven seasons led the Fighting Irish, encompasses the ten to twelve job changes Esco anticipated at the start of his own coaching career.

"In addition to the six types of coaches I've mentioned before," said Esco in a jovial mood, "we also had a seventh under Woody—the movie coach. The movie coach was charged with arranging a theatrical movie show for the Buckeyes on the night before games.

"The Friday night movie was an integral part of game preparation. Coach Hayes believed that a team either got better or worse, but never stayed the same. The pregame movies were a serious, last-minute means of motivating players and building team spirit in Woody's way of thinking.

"Before each game, the movie coach reviewed available films, show times, seating arrangements and transportation for Woody's approval. The movies also had to reflect his own inspirational and personal values—virtually impossible to meet week after week. Because of the risk of displeasing Woody, no one wanted to be the movie coach."

"Sark sure had this thankless job pegged," added Earle Bruce. "I was the movie coach when we were playing Minnesota one year. There were only two movies in town that fit our evening schedule—*Easy Rider* and a Walt Disney movie. When I went to finalize arrangements with Woody, I hold him that. 'The only choices, Coach, are *Easy Rider* and a Disney film.'

" 'What are the movies about?' he asked.

" 'I don't know, Coach, but I can tell you that some of the players really don't want to see the Disney movie.'

" 'OK, then, I guess its got to be *Easy Rider*.'

"When the team bus got back to the hotel, Woody asked Scooter McClain how the movie had gone. Scooter (an OSU assistant coach) said something to the effect that it was a horrible movie to show the team on the night before a game, all about bikers, drugs and dropping out—and I said to myself, 'thanks a lot, Scooter.'

"The next day the Buckeyes beat Minnesota by the score of 34-7. Because we had racked up larger scores in earlier games, Coach Hayes was searching for clues to what he saw as a decline in performance. In our staff meeting on the following Tuesday, he announced his conclusion.

" 'I know what the problem was—it was that damn movie, *Easy Rider*. We should have had a better movie to watch.'

"Then, to solve the problem, Woody acted on the spot: 'Earle, you're fired as movie coach!' "

As Woody Hayes approached the middle stages of his career, there emerged another thankless coaching position—the weather coach.

"When I was weather coach," said Bill Mallory, "it was my job to check the weather bureau every day for rain predictions. If there was a 60 percent chance of rain, I had to call the head grounds keeper to put down tarps to keep the field dry.

"Early in the week during our preparation for Minnesota, I drove by the field one evening, heading home. A storm was brewing and my order to put down the tarps had not been carried out. I returned to Woody's office and said:

" 'Coach, we got a problem.'

" 'What's that?'

" 'A storm's coming and the tarps aren't down.'

" 'Well, call the groundskeepers and get them down.'

" 'They've already gone for the day.'

" 'Then call the other coaches and get it done yourselves.'

"I started calling my colleagues and they began driving in to help. When I called Sark, he asked me to pick him up, but I said I didn't have the time. 'Why don't you call a cab and get down here by yourself,' I suggested."

" 'Oh, all right,' Sark grumbled.

"A driving rain storm hit and we wrassled with the tarps for about two and a half hours. We were slipping and sliding, and covered with mud. The craziness of putting down tarps to keep a wet field dry got to us, and we wound up laughing hilariously at ourselves and the pointlessness of our efforts—but Woody wanted the field covered.

"I used to get into some horrendous arguments with the head grounds keeper," continued Mallory, "who continually reminded me that putting tarps down was a sure way to kill the grass. And I kept telling him that I would much rather have the tarps kill the grass than have Woody kill me!"

Puzzled by this preoccupation with a dry playing surface, I asked Coach Mallory:

"Esco once told me a story, Bill, about the time Woody was adamant about practicing in the mud to prepare for Big Ten campaigns. The turf was so wet that the staff named the practice field Lake Hayes. When you say 'field,' do you mean the one in Ohio Stadium?"

"No, I mean the practice field—putting down tarps on the practice field. We always practiced on dry fields when I coached at Ohio State (1966 to 1968). Woody insisted on having a dry field."

"I wonder what caused the turnaround, because Esco's Lake Hayes story is just too preposterous for invention."

"I may know the answer," said Mallory: "I've heard that Woody attributed the loss of an important game to a sloppy practice field—a fine running back was injured while practicing in the mud. Woody concluded that losing a key back was the cause of losing the game."

"It would seem, then, that losing an actual game due to a muddy field was a lot more important than the hypothetical advantages of practicing on a sloppy field."

"Sounds reasonable to me," Mallory replied, "Woody hated to lose!"

Without Wheels

There is more to life than just the end zone.   *—Sark*

One morning while we were relaxing over coffee, Coach asked: "Do you know the name of the only modern-day OSU football coach who has never had an Ohio driver's license?"

This was a mystery to me and I told him so.

After letting me rack my brain for a moment or two, a smile slowly spread across his face:

"The answer is me, Esco Sarkkinen!"

This trivia question has frustrated Coach's players and friends for decades. The answer to the riddle has led to a lot of speculation because Esco never explained it. Not driving a car is simply unbelievable—as a rite of passage, every red-blooded young American can't wait to get a driver's license and a personal jalopy.

Not so for Esco, and this left me puzzled. I could only remember Coach walking or riding as a passenger in a car—never driving. Curious, I sometimes circled around his house through a back alley but never saw a car parked on his property. The only vehicle I ever saw was a small, dark blue pickup truck parked at the curb at odd hours. One day as I was driving by, Esco was sitting in the blue pickup with another person. It was Gene Fekete, his long-time friend and former colleague.

About a year later, Fekete and I were discussing Esco's trivia stories at the Buckeye Hall of Fame Cafe when the one about his not having a driver's license came up.

"Have you ever heard the full story?" Fekete asked.

"No, I haven't."

"Let me tell you. This trivia question dates from the time Sark was a student at OSU. He used to race around campus on a motor scooter. One day, Sark was late for a class in the physical education building and sped toward his usual parking spot behind the building, located on an

65

inclined loading ramp serving Townsend Hall. A milk truck with glass doors on the cargo box was backing up the ramp, loaded with milk cans.

"Rounding a corner blind, Sark saw the truck too late and lost control of his scooter. He hit the truck, smashed through a glass door, and wound up sprawled out in the midst of milk cans, broken glass, and spilled milk. It was pure luck that Esco wasn't killed or seriously injured. As a result of this terrifying crash, Esco lost the desire to drive any vehicle, including an automobile.

"Because Sark gave up driving permanently, I became one of his taxi drivers when we coached together—and later after we both retired."

"As a faculty member," recalls defensive coach George Hill, "Sark was eligible for a class A parking sticker, even though he didn't drive. Every year, he made deals with Buckeye players who owned a car—they got the best reserved parking privileges on campus in exchange for giving Sark free taxi service around campus."

Recruiting

If you can't run with the big dogs, join the puppies on the porch.   —Sark

"Sark was pretty straightforward as a recruiter," Bo Schembechler remembered. "He was not fancy or flashy. His basic pitch to recruits was this:

" 'Take a look at Ohio State. It has the best coaches. It has the best players. It has the best program—and you can also get a good education. If you want the best, why would you want to go anywhere but Ohio State?'

"If a recruit couldn't see the merit in this argument, Sark was of the opinion that he probably wasn't a player the Bucks wanted anyway."

"Sark did not drive and this made it difficult for him to recruit the Cleveland area," former assistant coach Lou McCullough recalled, "and when I was put in charge of recruiting in 1963, I

reallocated area responsibilities. I took Cincinnati and gave Cleveland to Coach Larry Catuzzi. Esco was given Columbus and Central Ohio where he could get the driving help he needed to call on potential players and high school coaches. Sark was a terrific recruiter and we got our share of talent from the Columbus area."

"While Sark was coaching," according to Gene Fekete, "his wife, Freda, drove him to the office or classes in the morning and I would drive him

Greg Lashutka and Esco Sarkkinen

68

home in the afternoon. There were many times when Freda drove Sark on recruiting trips around the Columbus area—so you might say Ohio State had an unusual husband-wife recruiting team."

"Coach Sarkkinen was a low-key recruiter," explained Greg Lashutka, "quite a contrast to some of his more aggressive, fast-talking counterparts. I was impressed by Sark's family background, immigrants like my own, and his origins in northeast Ohio. My family and I were taken by the way he modestly explained the advantages of attending Ohio State. I decided I wanted to play for Esco.

"When we suited up for our first day of practice, Esco took us out into the vast emptiness of Ohio Stadium, and said:

" 'I'd like all of you to line up against the wall here, about midfield, and tell me what you hear.'

"We were puzzled by his instructions but did what Sark asked. When we heard nothing, we told him so."

" 'You're not listening carefully enough. Try listening more carefully.'

"Again we couldn't hear a thing.

"After another round or two like this, I was beginning to wonder how I had been persuaded to come play for this strange-acting character.

"Sark then asked us to give it one more try, this time at our attentive best. After several minutes of silence, we heard him quietly whisper the following words in a five-beat cadence:

" 'Let's...go...with...Es...co!

" 'Let's...go...with...Es...co!

" 'Let's...go...with...Es...co!'

"The tension of our first practice was quickly dispelled."

"One year, Coach Hayes and the rest of the staff left Columbus on a train eastbound for the American Football Coaches Association convention," said Sark. "Most of us looked upon a trip like this as a chance to relax, have a few drinks together, and swap stories.

"When the train pulled into a small station in eastern Ohio, Woody looked out the window and spotted a familiar name on the station sign. He turned to us and said:

" 'We've been trying to recruit an outstanding player from this area...I think I'll get off here and see if I can talk to him and his parents...all of you go ahead without me. Take my baggage to the hotel and I'll catch up with you later on the next train.'

"Coach Hayes hopped off the train and enthusiastically went in search of his prized recruit. Getting the players needed to win was one of his highest priorities, much higher than socializing... Woody believed that you win with people and lived this belief."

"Sark used taxicabs to seek out talent for the Buckeyes," said Bill Mallory. "We used to say that if you see a empty cab standing in front of a high school building in Columbus, Sark is probably inside recruiting."

Work Ethic

Moderation in all things.—Buddhist aphorism

Nothing succeeds like excess.—Oscar Wilde

"Members of the OSU coaching staff were relaxing in Coach Hayes' office one day, talking philosophically about coaching," Sark recalled.

"Reflecting on his own success, Woody said: 'I don't think I'm a genius or great mind when it comes to football. Basically, I get a lot of ideas from other coaches. I observe what they do, take the best from them, and use them myself. The way I win is by working harder!' "

While addressing a commencement audience in 1968, Woody Hayes said he had always found people bigger, faster, harder or smarter than himself. He then posed a question about his competitors, and proceeded to answer it himself:

72

"But you know what they couldn't do?

"They couldn't out-work me—they couldn't out-work me. And I ran into coaches…who had a much better background than I did, (who) knew a lot more about football than I did, but they couldn't work as long as I could. They couldn't stick in there as long as I could…

"And I had a great, great association with my coaches. There was no one who ever had better people than I did—or better players—and we outworked them."

"Ohio State had the hardest working coaching staff around," Lou McCullough testified, "working long hours, seven days a week during the season.

"After a Saturday afternoon game in Ohio Stadium, for instance, we would get game films back around 6 p.m. With dinner already out of the way, we would grade films into the night, wrapping up around 11 p.m. On Sunday morning, the staff would reassemble around 8 a.m. to review game results and lay the foundation for the upcoming game, deciding on the adjustments we would make. We usually worked late on Sunday, finishing up around 11 p.m.

"On weekdays, the coaching staff generally began work at 7:45 a.m. and finished between 10 and 11 p.m.

"Meetings and practices on Monday and Tuesday were similar, aimed at individual instruction to correct mistakes and teach the adjustments for the upcoming game. Some time on Monday was always given to preparation for the Michigan game, and occasionally some other key game. A scheduled staff meeting was usually held on Monday evening and sometimes on Tuesday.

"Wednesday and Thursday practices were devoted to game preparation, often with heavy work and contact. The staff worked in the office Wednesday evenings, sometimes long into the night.

"Thursday evenings we usually spent at home— working, of course. This was the time devoted to recruiting calls and contacting prospects, from around 7 to 11 p.m. At my house, it was also movie night. I used to bring home game films for the upcoming game, thread them onto a projector, make popcorn, and let my kids take over while I made my calls. They loved to play with the projector, running films forward and backward until time for bed. Then, I would look at them myself before turning in.

"A light workout on Friday focused on all phases of the kicking game, followed by a team dinner and movie. On Saturday, we played another game and started all over again.

"Because Sark coached defensive ends and scouted opponents, I got to know him very well. We worked together in shared office space but had little time for socializing. Most of our social time occurred at lunch or out of town. Esco and I turned out to be the best of friends and I often visited with him and his family after 1970, my last season at OSU."

"I learned more about football from Esco Sarkkinen than from any other coach in my career." —*George Hill, defensive coach*

75

Paying Forward

The game is more than the players of the
game, and the ship is more than the crew.
—Rudyard Kipling

"A motivating force behind the Buckeyes is the principle of *paying forward*," according to Greg Lashutka, "and Esco Sarkkinen is the best example I have ever known.

"The principle of paying forward set the standard for our primary responsibilities as team members. It originated with Ralph Waldo Emerson, who wrote: 'You can pay back only seldom… (but)…you can always pay forward and you must pay line for line, deed for deed, and cent for cent.' In terms of fashioning a satisfying life, the basic idea here is to be grateful for all that comes our way—family, friends, education, recognition—and reinvest them in others, to improve the future.

"As players, we were urged to train hard, practice hard, play hard, and study hard in order to make this larger contribution—we were obliged to develop our abilities to the maximum. We were also taught that it was necessary to sacrifice for the team and the greater good. Excellence demanded choices regarding how we would spend our time and energies."

"While Coach Hayes was a staunch, vocal advocate of paying forward, mentioning this principle in nearly every speech he ever gave, Coach Sarkkinen quietly demonstrated what it meant every day on the practice field. We all became aware of Sark's exceptional willingness to invest his time, talent, and experience in his position players and the team.

"The Buckeyes have become a special fraternity because of their willingness to pay forward. Knowing of my own exposure to this principle, it should come as no surprise that public service has been the focal point of my life for nearly thirty years—and that Esco Sarkkinen became a life-long friend," said Lashutka, an end and team captain who later served as mayor of Columbus.

Scouting

Hear all, see all, say nothing.
—Admiral Cannaris

One morning at Mill Street Bagels, Coach was reminiscing about the 1952 OSU-Illinois game which the Bucks won 27 to 7. Our tablemate Doug, who had played in the game for Ohio State, expressed his wonder at the value of Sark's scouting contribution:

"Do you recall, Sark, that you had noticed an Illinois lineman with the habit of lining up with his feet parallel to the line of scrimmage for a pass play or dropping one foot back slightly for a running play?"

"Yes, I remember that…"

"And briefing me in practice during the week before the game?"

"Sure do…"

"Well, while making defensive calls (as a linebacker), I kept my eyes on this opposing player's feet. Your information was accurate on every play during the first half and helped us shut down

78

Sark on a scouting assignment

the Illini offense—on every down we knew what type of play they were going to run. After the half, I got bold and began calling out 'pass' or 'run' for our side to hear. My teammates questioned me, but I assured them I was calling plays according to your instructions.

"Late in the third quarter, Tommy O'Connell (an All-American quarterback) finally reached his boiling point. The Illini broke their huddle and lined up, and just before O'Connell started his count, I called out 'pass.' Across the line, a frustrated O'Connell stopped his count and barked:

" 'How in the hell do you know that?'

" 'There's someone on your side tipping me off,' I said with a monstrous grin.

"Of course, the lineman couldn't change an ingrained habit, even if he was aware of it, and I continued to call out 'pass' or 'run' reliably. The games' outcome was sealed when an Illinois pass was intercepted after another accurate defensive call, leading to a final Buckeye touchdown.

"It sure was a lot of fun for the defense to go on the offense with your information!"

"Against Wisconsin, our record was twenty-five wins, one loss and one tie during the years I coached," said Coach, "and scouting played a crucial role.

"Through scouting, our staff learned that Wisconsin had the habit of installing its offense gradually rather than all at once prior to the beginning of each season. As we usually played the Badgers early in the season, the 'tendency book' we compiled on them was accurate and reliable. The teams facing the Badgers later on in the season were playing a much less predictable and better prepared football team.

"During one four-year period, we observed that Wisconsin's powerful All-American running back, Alan Ameche, either carried the ball or blocked on every play. So, in preparing for the Badgers, we drilled our linebackers to key on Ameche on every play because he was sure to be in the vicinity of the ball. Against Ohio State, Ameche never had one of the outstanding rushing days which marked his career.

"Years later, members of the UCLA and OSU coaching staffs compared scouting notes on Wisconsin and learned that we both had discovered the same tendencies. We recalled living in fear that our insights into Wisconsin's game would become known, thereby losing a game day advantage."

"While I was scouting other teams," Sark remarked, "it was impossible to grasp the action by focusing on individual players. You had to train yourself to observe and register the actions of all twenty-two players at one time, eliminating eye movement entirely.

"To do this I had to develop what I call a *relaxed stare,* a technique useful in grasping the entire field as a whole. While in this mode, it is possible to be aware of important action in the vicinity of the ball handler. By observing in this way, it is possible to grasp and record the gist of each play.

"I cultivated this visual skill through a WW II

aircraft spotter program developed at OSU for the military by Hoyt Sherman, a fine arts professor. The professor conceived and built a special research-teaching studio with large screens, a projector and a mechanical flasher—nicknamed the 'flash lab' by students. In it, we were taught to reach out and seize visual images aggressively, as distinct from the normal act of casual viewing."

Professor Sherman wrote at the time:

"Most sports—notably football, basketball, baseball, hockey, soccer, tennis and handball—require a high degree of visual skill if competency is to be achieved in the sport. The good player must be able to see the whole visual field in which the play is emerging, and he must see most of it as peripheral vision, out of the corner of his eye."

Flash lab results were astounding. In a short period, peripheral vision and depth judgments improved dramatically while reaction times dropped significantly.

"By applying Professor Sherman's teaching to scouting," Coach continued, "I found it possible to sketch the major offensive and defensive tendencies of all the teams we were scheduled to meet. A locker full of information accumulated on the teams I was assigned to scout, helping to prepare the Buckeyes year after year.

"Gathering team information once was a press box-type activity, observing with binoculars and diagramming with pad and pencil. While all of the old methods have been supplanted by camera, film, tape and rapid printing, the original intelligence function of scouting still remains."

Pandel Savic, quarterback from 1947 to 1949, remembers the flash lab exercises vividly:

"In a large dark room, we stood with large sheets of paper on a stand and a charcoal stick in our hand. Professor Sherman then flashed images on a large screen at the front of room. The exposure time was gradually reduced to an incredible one tenth of a second. After each image was flashed, the lights were turned on and we had to sketch what we had visualized.

"Of course, there was no time to study the images in detail, which is what we do in the course of normal seeing. You had to train yourself to record your whole field of vision in a split-second glance—and remember it well enough to put it down on paper.

"What Esco calls a *relaxed stare,* I describe as *scanning,* because this is what a quarterback has to do. You might begin a pass play with a primary receiver in mind but you still have to scan the field to be aware of where all the other receivers are going to be and make a decision on where to throw the ball. We actually took flash lab lessons and applied them to the passing game, at the urging of Coach Sarkkinen.

"The quarterbacks in field applications were Pete Perini, Bucky Wertz, Bill Peterson and myself. The receivers we worked with were Dick Schnittker, Ralph Armstrong, Jan Hague and Tom Watson. The coaches were Wes Fesler, Esco, and Dick Fisher, the quarterback coach.

"Special quarterback helmets were made for us. Each helmet had a special visor equipped with a shutter that was tripped manually with long strings. The helmets were designed so we had about a tenth of a second or so to read the patterns receivers were running. When the shutter was closed you couldn't see anything.

"Each quarterback had a receiver with a different colored jersey—red, green, blue and yellow, as I recall. The receivers ran patterns simultaneously. When the shutters opened on our

A couple of quarterbacks try out the "flash lab"

helmets for a split second, we each had to pick out our own receiver and throw to where we figured he would be when the ball arrived.

"When we first began, our completions were very low, around ten percent. Gradually, we built up our visual skills to where completion percentages were in the forty to fifty percent range. The skills we developed were taken into game situations and proved effective. The theory and principles behind effective scanning, or relaxed staring, were published in *Popular Mechanics*."

"I believe that TV announcers are way off base," Coach insisted, "when they criticize a quarterback for not being able to spot primary and secondary receivers successively. In the game situation there is not enough time to look off from one receiver to a second and then a third or more, particularly in today's game.

"At the highest level of play, it is more likely that the quarterback will take the snap, start reading all receivers simultaneously, and decide to throw to the one he believes will be breaking into the clear when the ball arrives.

"Bob Hoying's touchdown throw to Rickey Dudley in the 1995 Penn State game is a good illustration of this—the ball was released by Hoying when defenders were still between Dudley and the goal line.

"I should also mention that Rickey was the fastest man on the Buckeye squad. This fact was successfully hidden from Penn State and other opponents who concentrated more on defending against Rickey's leaping ability which he developed playing basketball."

"Occasionally Esco and I scouted together at the same time," said Gene Fekete, "when two upcoming opponents were playing each other. We executed our scouting assignments under the pressure of high expectations. Coach Hayes was very demanding when it came to scouting.

"When we returned from scouting trips, his first question was certain to be: 'Can we beat 'em?'

The next question was: 'How?' The Old Man wanted a straight answer—yes or no—and would not tolerate any hedging on our part. He was not interested in knowing whether or not the Buckeyes could be competitive, he was interested in whether or not we could win—and how we could do it!"

Bill Mallory recalls: "Esco Sarkkinen loved to scout other teams. On one of my open weekends, he invited me to go along on a scouting trip with him, in a small plane as usual. When we flew into a large storm I lost my enthusiasm for scouting. But it was instructive to observe the organized way in which Sark scouted an opponent. He was the best at game analysis and prediction, offensively and defensively. Some of us jokingly speculated that it was scouting that helped Sark forge a long-term relationship with Woody Hayes—after all, scouting gave him nine out-of-town trips each season."

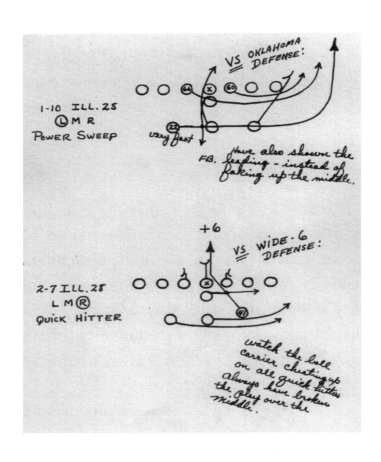

A sample of a scouting report,
illustrating plays as run during
a game by an upcoming opponent

"Today, it's hard to appreciate the exceptional scouting skills of Sark," said Bill Arnsparger, a former assistant coach, coming off a consulting assignment with the Washington Redskins. "Decades ago, Sark was turning out scouting reports the equivalent of what we're able to achieve today with tapes, television, instant replays, instant cameras, and more eyes on the field. It's simply amazing that Sark could do a comparable job alone by working two or three live games by himself.

"Perhaps unknown to many Buckeye fans, Sark had a nationwide reputation within the coaching profession as one of the best scouts in the business, some would even say the best. His standing as a scouting coach was on a par with his professional stature as a fine end coach. Because personal scouting has since been superseded by the exchange of game films, a change instituted by NCAA rules, it's now difficult to appreciate the edge Sark gave to the Buckeyes."

In his 1957 book, *Football at Ohio State,* Woody Hayes quoted Esco as saying: "A good scouting job is worth 13 points to the team."

Bo Schembechler waxed enthusiastic about Sark's scouting ability:

"You can't imagine how critically important scouting was during Woody's era. No exchange of films. No tapes. No replays. The only thing allowed was just one man, sitting above the crowd, ferreting out the strengths, weaknesses and tendencies of an opponent—what an awesome responsibility!

"Sark was acknowledged as the best football scout in the Big Ten, certainly, and probably in the country. I can't emphasize how much a good scout meant to our (OSU) football program when I was an assistant coach—it was a critical resource."

Greg Lashutka also attested to the advantage Sark gave to the Buckeyes.

"For certain, Esco Sarkkinen was a major factor in the NCAA changing its rules to prohibit the use of personal scouts in collegiate football."

Dean Dugger, an All-American end who played under Sark on the 1954 national championship team, recalls the legendary, meticulous preparation with which Coach carried out his responsibilities:

"Esco Sarkkinen was head scout and had an uncanny, intuitive sense for the game of football. Sark always scouted our toughest opponents, including Michigan and Wisconsin. When we were preparing for one game with the Badgers, he cautioned:

"Be alert, Dugger! Wisconsin has an effective fake punt play. They've only run it once this year and it was very successful. I think they may have been holding back in their last few games. If the situation is right, I have a feeling that they might try to spring a fake punt on us.

"Late in the game, Wisconsin had the ball in

their own territory. Since we played both ways in '54, I was getting pretty tired as the second half ground on. The scoreboard showed that we were comfortably ahead. I was tempted to ditch my defensive assignment and take a breather by staying home, instead of running a looping stunt called for in punting situations—saving energy for when we went on offense.

"But then I thought of Esco's admonition. The Badgers were fourth and short near their own forty yard line. They were behind and would not want to turn the ball over. It was an ideal situation to fake a punt. As I rapidly mulled over the situation, I said 'no' to myself—'I better put out the full effort on this fourth-down play.'

"The Badgers faked a punt and ran the ball. By reacting defensively the way Sark suggested, I was in a perfect position to stop the Badgers' ball carrier.

"This anecdote illustrates how thoroughly Coach Sarkkinen prepared us for our toughest opponents. He always had us ready to play. When he was scouting, he could grasp what was happening and pick out the key details. He just didn't fly with hunches, he checked them out. Whenever Sark did the scouting on an upcoming opponent, I was confident that the Bucks would be properly prepared.

"As our position coach, Sark prompted us to start thinking the way he did: What is the situation? What is the other team likely to do? What sort of action should I be ready to take? Anticipation and thinking were watchwords of his coaching.

"My older brother, Jack, who also played for Coach Sarkkinen, was an All-American end on the 1944 national championship team. Sark used to refer to us as the Dugger Boys. Even though he was Finnish, I often referred to Sark as the Smiling Swede—because most of the time there was an infectious smile on his face. I would also point out that Sark was a very diplomatic person. He avoided taking unkind or judgmental positions on players and coaches—he was an accepting person."

"Have I ever told you the story of Ralphie, the buffalo?"

"No," I said, wondering what a buffalo had to do with college football, and could hardly wait to find out. Coach began with a grin:

"Colorado had a buffalo for a mascot, affectionately called 'Ralphie.' Originally, the mascot had been named 'Ralph' by the students when adopted as a calf. However, when their new mascot grew up to be a female, 'his' name was changed to 'Ralphie.' I saw Ralphie several times when I flew out to Boulder to scout the Buffalos.

"Ralphie was specially schooled for a single act in pregame ceremonies. Just before kickoff, Ralphie was wheeled out to the Colorado end zone in a large cage. Then she was released and led the Buffs onto the playing field.

"Ralphie was trained to gallop one hundred yards to the opposite end zone, turn around, gallop back another hundred yards, and retire to the cage—like a horse returning to its barn. Cowboy-attired cheerleaders, stetsons flopping and flying, enlivened the spectacle by hanging on to Ralphie's harness and trying to run with her, spurring the home town crowd into a pregame frenzy.

"Running Ralphie was one of the funniest scenes I have ever witnessed in college football. It gave me an idea on how to have a little fun of my own when Colorado came to play in Ohio Stadium.

"When the Buffalos were here, I had to go out of town to scout an upcoming opponent. Before leaving, I gave a fictitious message to my senior equipment manager to be delivered to Coach Eddie Crowder in the Colorado dressing room, just before the game. He was instructed to say:

" 'Coach Hayes is concerned about Ralphie running up and down the playing field dropping buffalo chips all along the way. He hopes you will be considerate enough to clean up after Ralphie so the Buckeyes won't have to roll around in buffalo crap all afternoon.'

"Just before kickoff, my equipment manager went to the Buffs' dressing room and informed his counterpart that he had a message for Coach Crowder from Coach Hayes. Crowder was just starting his pregame inspirational speech when interrupted to take my bogus message from

Woody. He found the timing unbelievable but left a room full of tense players to come out and take the message anyway.

"My equipment manager promptly relayed the

Ralphie on the rampage

message about cleaning up the buffalo crap left on the field after Ralphie was done running.

"Eddie Crowder's searing remarks are best left unprinted but you can imagine their off-color intensity when he spotted the ruse—Ralphie never performed at away games due to the difficulties of transporting a beast of her size!

"My manager immediately realized that he too had been taken in, and while still verbally blistered, had a few choice words for me when I returned to Columbus. I still catch myself laughing when I imagine Crowder blowing his top.

"Do you have any regrets, Coach?"

"Not really—only a minor one."

"What's that?"

"As head scout I never got to see the Buckeyes play, because I was out of town scouting. The only times I attended Ohio State games was when we played Michigan or went to a bowl game.

"My only regret is that I couldn't be with my players on game day."

99

That Team Up North

Football...combines the two worst aspects of American life. It is violence punctuated by committee meetings. —George Will

Displaying mild exasperation from recent losses (in the 1990's) to the Wolverines, Coach elaborated on an old-time formula for putting more check marks in the win column:

"When I was coaching, the Big Ten was often called The Big Two and The Little Eight because of the dominance of Ohio State and Michigan. Coach Hayes always figured that the Buckeyes would have three tough games on their schedule and Michigan was always regarded as the toughest. This expectation shaped our approach to the entire football season.

"In spring practice, Coach Hayes would begin to install the offensive plays designed for the big game and run them daily against our simulation of the Wolverine defense. Much of spring practice was dedicated to preparing for Michigan. Fall practice would continue with the same steady, intense concentration, relieved only by preparation for a couple of other challenging opponents.

"Even when the Buckeyes began playing conference games, a lot of weekly practice time was spent preparing for Michigan. For weaker opponents, our practice time was minimal—Coach Hayes figured that Ohio State always had the talent and depth to compete effectively. In short, if the Buckeyes were prepared to play Michigan, they could beat the other Big Ten teams.

"Michigan was always regarded as the stepping stone to the Big Ten title and the Rose Bowl, and Coach Hayes never forgot it. His record against Michigan was sixteen wins, eleven losses and one tie. During his tenure as head coach, he won or shared the Big Ten Championship thirteen times in twenty eight seasons. It is hard to argue with the way he prepared for each season.

"Today, there is more balance in the Big Ten so it is no longer the Big Two and Little Eight, and there are more than a couple of teams that can beat you. Even so, many old timers like me still believe it takes exceptional preparation to beat that Team Up North."

The scoreboard says it all!

Esco addresses the Senior Tackle,
before the Michigan game

"Sark certainly is correct regarding the emphasis Coach Hayes placed on winning the Michigan game," said Earle Bruce. "Michigan truly was THE GAME. It was never out of Woody's thoughts—or ours—for good reason.

"It was a different era back then, a time of risky one-year contracts. We all understood that if we lost three straight games to the Wolverines, Coach Hayes and the rest of us would be out looking for work. If you don't believe me, look at the three years prior to Woody's dismissal.

"Leading up to the Gator Bowl, the Buckeyes had three solid seasons (and close to a 70 percent won-loss ratio). They were co-champions twice and went to the Orange and Sugar bowls. At many schools, this would have been an enviable record—but not at Ohio State, when it included three straight losing efforts against Michigan. The lesson was not lost on me when I took over as head coach.

"Basically, I adopted Woody's year 'round approach to the Michigan game, starting game preparation during spring practice. Based on film analysis, we began conceiving or selecting plays we thought would work well against the Wolverines, including a few new pass plays they had never seen. We began running these plays in spring practice and whenever we could find some time in the fall.

"The special emphasis I placed on game preparation was preparing and motivating each Buckeye to do individual battle with the player he would have to face on every play—and not to think about the game as a whole. If each one of our players could win his own individual battle, I emphasized, the team could expect to win!"

"When I went to Michigan in 1963," explained Bo Schembechler, I had a coaching staff without Big Ten experience. The first thing I told them was this: 'The objective of our entire season is to beat Ohio State.'

"The Buckeyes were the dominant team of the era, racking up many titles, national championships and bowl appearances. My attitude toward the Buckeyes was similar to Woody Hayes' reasoning on the Wolverines: If we could beat Ohio State, Michigan would be in shape to compete with any other team in the Big Ten.

"Our preparation was equally as intense and continuous as that in Columbus. Ohio State was always on our mind. Every day we did something to get ready for the Buckeyes.

"For instance, I installed Ohio State's premier off-tackle play—26 and 27—in the Wolverine offense. I did this so our defense would really understand the off-tackle play and how to defend against it. So, under the guise of practicing our own offense, we learned how to defend the Buckeye's best play—so there wouldn't be any surprises on game day.

"The intense preparation and desire to win were what made the Ohio State-Michigan game so great! We both knew a lot about each other and we both prepared year-round. When the game itself was played, it was usually a knock-down, drag-out affair—a real dog fight.

"The Big Game invariably came down to mental attitude, determination, stamina, and effort. Winning was a matter of how perfectly you could play the game as a team, how the great players rose to the occasion, and how much you wanted the win. That's what made the Ohio State-Michigan game so special. It went on like this year after year. No other rivalry compared to Ohio State-Michigan."

"What is often overlooked," explained Earle Bruce, "is that famous rivalries like Ohio State-Michigan are great because each team has a good chance of winning—and everyone knows it!"

Intrigued by Earle's comment, I checked the won-lost records of the OSU-Michigan games during Sark's 32-year coaching career. Coach Bruce was right. Sixty percent of the time, the winning team one year lost or tied the next year! The longest winning streak put together by either team was four straight wins by OSU under Woody Hayes from 1960 to 1963. Michigan put together three straight wins from 1946 through

1948 and again from 1976 through 1978. Other than these streaks, only Ohio State was able to score back-to-back wins. Woody did it four times.

Woody was 16-11-1 against the Wolverines—a 59 percent winning average, a sharp contrast to his overall Big Ten record of 79 percent. Bruce was 5-4-0 against Michigan—56 percent—even though he won 82 percent of all his Big Ten contests. Bo Schembechler wound up 11-9-1 against the Buckeyes—a 55 percent winning rate, compared to an overall 85 percent winning ratio against all Big Ten opponents.

Coach Bruce concluded: "With each squad having an even chance of winning, there was enormous tension and suspense in the Ohio State-Michigan game. Championships, rankings, and major bowl bids were often on the line. And at the end of a tough season, all of these rewards hung by a single, precarious thread. It's no wonder that rivalry victories were dramatic and memorable."

1968

The past was more glorious: 'football magic' was in the air. I'm not so sure that it was. —*Sark, commenting on 1968*

"How do you think the Bucks will do this season, Coach?" I asked one morning.

"I don't know," he replied, "I never try to predict the outcome of a football season, and I'll tell you why.

"As was customary at the beginning of each season, we coaches, gathered around Coach Hayes' office desk, were asked for our individual predictions for 1968—by secret ballot. When the ballots were opened, the best prediction I recall was 7-2-1.

"The 1968 Buckeye team went 10-0, won the Big Ten championship, and became national champions by beating Southern California in the Rose Bowl.

"So, you never really know what kind of team you've got until you start playing games. We've had some teams with enormous talent but they never seemed to jell. How hard we worked didn't seem to make any difference. I don't know why some teams live up to their potential and others fail. If I had the answer, it might be possible to make predictions."

"The 1968 season was perfect but the events leading up to this season were less than memorable," according to Bill Mallory, one of Sark's colleagues at the time.

"The Buckeyes won 4 and dropped 5 in 1966 including a loss to Michigan, finishing sixth in the Big Ten. In 1967, our record improved to 6 and 4, and we beat Michigan, but wound up fourth in the Big Ten. The dark cloud on 1967 was a 41-6 pasting by Purdue, setting the stage for the 1968 season. The Boilermakers were the preseason favorites to repeat as Big Ten champions.

"Coach Hayes came to the early conclusion that the Purdue game, our Big Ten opener, was the key to a successful 1968 season and began to plan accordingly. The approach we took was similar to the intense, steady preparation made for Michigan. Whenever there were blocks of practice and study time available, we prepared for Purdue—beginning in spring practice.

"Our defensive coaches threw themselves into the preparation effort. For instance, all the offensive plays from nine or ten Purdue game films were charted and analyzed by Lou (McCullough, the defensive coordinator). Around 15 to 16 of the Boilermaker's best plays were identified—half running and half passing, plus a few kicking plays. Film clips of these plays were then spliced by Lou into one study film. Copies of this film and play charts were distributed to members of the defensive staff just after the spring game. Our defensive goal was to take away all of Purdue's best plays.

"We studied the Purdue offense thoroughly through the summer and met together often. It was here that I really began to appreciate Sark. Lou (Holtz) and I were the young, enthusiastic coaches bursting with ideas to discuss. Sark was the experienced veteran who had been with Woody more than fifteen years. He was a thinker more than a talker, and if you wanted to know what he was thinking, you had to ask. When a question was put to Sark, he would take his time to think it through before answering—slowly puffing on his cigarette. Then he would answer very deliberately. None of us ever took Sark's comments lightly.

"Woody was looking over our shoulders the entire summer. The Purdue game was always in the forefront. While directing the offensive preparations, he somehow found the time to pop in and out of our defensive meetings. Whenever discussing game preparations with us, he would listen to all the more vocal, animated members of the defensive staff. But then, you could count on him to say: 'What do you think, Sark?' And he would patiently wait while Sark took a few cigarette puffs before replying. It was obvious that Woody relied on Sark's judgment.

"The summer had its funny moments, as I look back on them. For instance, when we went to alumni golf outings and other social functions, Woody invariably asked us to show up early— and to bring along a movie projector, or to stop back at the office, to review Purdue films. He was that determined to win the Purdue game, using every spare moment available. By the end of the summer, there was little that we didn't know about the Boilermakers, and we began fall practice sharply focused on our BigTen opener.

"Purdue came into the Ohio State game ranked number one nationally and the solid favorite, averaging a little over forty points in their previous games. Mike Phipps at quarterback and an outstanding halfback, Leroy Keyes, powered the Boilermakers. Phipps was intercepted twice under pressure, by Ted Provost and Jim Stillwagon, leading to Buckeye touchdowns. Keyes was held to around twenty yards, effectively shut down by Jack Tatum. The Buckeyes beat the Boilermakers by the score of 13-0, and Coach Hayes credited the OSU defense for this superlative victory.

"After opening wins over SMU and Oregon, the win over Purdue brought national attention to the Buckeyes while launching their undefeated runs for the Big Ten and national championships."

Rose Bowl

He threw a Lady Godiva pass—it had nothing on it!   *—Sark*

"When we were facing Southern California in the '69 Rose Bowl," Coach explained, "our main concern was containing O.J. Simpson. Although widely known for his open-field running, he was also powerful and fast—a first-class sprinter. The general expectation of opponents was that USC would run its famous Student Body Left or Student Body Right plays to the wide side of the field to leverage Simpson's speed.

"Our scouting showed otherwise. Southern Cal did not hesitate to run O.J. to the short side of the field, often leading to long gains and scores. We reasoned that the Trojans would stick with this successful short-side tendency.

"Playing an unbalanced line on defense, we put All-American Jack Tatum—the Monster Man— on the wide side of the field to contain Simpson. We also adjusted our line and linebacker play to add strength to the weak side of the field. The Bucks were able to keep Simpson in check in the first half, except for one play.

"When one of our first-half punts went into the USC end zone, it was downed and brought out to the twenty yard line. With the ball smack in the middle of the field, we had no clues on how to line up. We figured one way and Southern California went the other. Simpson streaked 80 yards for a quick score, igniting the partisan hometown crowd. The Trojans added a field goal to take a 10-0 lead. But the Bucks battled back and tied the score by halftime."

Lou McCullough, then defensive coach, remembers the situation: "I was working the game from the press box at the time O.J. scored. For just such an occurrence, however, we came into the Rose Bowl with alternative defensive plans—and made some adjustments at half time. We called on Mark Stier, one of our linebackers, to 'mirror' O.J. in the second half—that is, do exactly what Simpson was doing but on our side of the line. This defensive adjustment strengthened our linebacker-safety play considerably because we now had Tatum and Stier both pursuing Simpson.

"The Buckeyes bounced back and put 17 points on the board in the second half. If USC had not scored a controversial touchdown as the game was about to end, the Trojans would have been scoreless in the second half. Outside his long touchdown run, we held O.J. to less than a hundred yards for the day—not a bad effort against the Heisman Trophy winner."

"Winning this Rose Bowl game was particularly sweet," said Esco, "because the Buckeyes and Trojans had been ranked one and two throughout the 1968 season and we were able to put the final touches on a perfect season."

"It's really sad," Coach reflected, "when you stop to think about O.J. and all of his talent that has gone to waste. He had it all: athletic star, successful actor endorsements, probably more than enough money. It's sad because O.J. was admired—really looked up to in the black community.

"One day before the game, we were scheduled to practice on the Rose Bowl field right after USC. The Buckeyes dressed early and drifted onto the field before the Trojans were finished. When we (coaches) got to the field, we were concerned—clusters of Buckeye players were standing on the sidelines in awe as O.J. ran through practice plays. The admiration of our players was obvious.

"We were concerned that admiration could lead to intimidation, and effect us on game day. So we stepped up talk about the Trojans being players that we could compete with—they were not invincible and they could be beat. As it turned out, our concerns were unfounded.

"While we were dressing after the game, O.J. appeared in the Buckeye dressing room in his game uniform, still sweaty and dirty. He circulated through the dressing room to congratulate the Buckeyes on their victory and individual play. Among other comments, I heard him say: 'Today was the best linebacking I've ever run against.'

"O.J. was such a gentleman on that day," Coach said with a tinge of disappointment and compassion.

Gene Fekete, Hilo Hatti, and Esco cut loose

"Esco and Freda used the Rose Bowl games to organize family Christmas celebrations," said their daughter, Sandy. "Our doors and rooms were always decorated for the holidays and exchanging presents was traditional. Since OSU went to nine Rose Bowl games when I was growing up, we had many marvelous mid-winter vacations in sunny California.

"We often came home with mementos which I

have treasured over the years. I still have an inlaid Rose Bowl fruit plate which graced my parents' table for years and a necklace with a gold medallion that is similar to the face of a Rose Bowl game ring."

"The Rose Bowl Committee arranged for each coach to have a brand new automobile during the Buckeye's stay in Pasadena," related Sandy. "As Esco didn't drive, he let his players use his car until the family arrived. Then, the car belonged to Freda and me. One year we got a gold Lincoln Continental—quite a boat.

"One of the coach's wives and I decided to get dressed up and go out on New Year's Eve rather than hang around at our staid hotel. We put on our best short-skirted suits, heels, and jewelry, and went to Disneyland on the other side of Los Angeles. On our way home, after midnight, we got lost and I pulled into a deserted gas station to check our map. We were in a rough neighborhood and anxious to be on our way.

"To our dismay, a car slowly rolled up behind us and stopped—but we were relieved when bubble lights on top the car began flashing. It was the police. The officer driving the cruiser got out, slowly walked up from the rear, tapped on my window, and motioned for me to open it:

" 'Good evening, ladies,' he said with exaggerated courtesy, 'how are the two of you this lovely night?'

" 'Real good, officer.'

" 'This sure is a mighty fine car you have.'

" 'Yes, it is.'

" 'Kind of late to be out driving around, isn't it?'

" 'Yes...'

" 'You two sure are dolled up for the night. Do you mind telling me where you're going?'

" 'No sir, we're just going back to our hotel, we're on our way home from Disneyland.'

" 'Sure you are. Just wait here a minute, ladies, I want my partner to hear this for himself.'

" 'Okay,' I said, and turned to my companion.

" 'These cops think we're hookers out cruising for johns and want to have a little fun with us...I'm married to a cop, so let me handle this.'

119

"When the officers again approached us, the second one asked through my window, 'Well now, ladies, where did you get this terrific set of wheels?'

" 'The car is a loaner from the Rose Bowl committee,' I replied, 'my dad is a coach for the Ohio State Buckeyes and we get to use it until we return to Columbus.'

" 'Is that so?' the officer asked with amused skepticism.

" 'Yes sir, it is.'

" 'Perhaps you'd like to show me your driver's license.'

"I got out my Ohio driver's license and when the the officer saw my name—Sandra Sue Hayes— his jaw went slack. As he stepped back, I could almost hear the wheels spinning in his head: Ohio State...Rose Bowl...Woody Hayes...Sandra Hayes...incident...MEDIA!

" 'Oh my God,' I overhead heard him say to his partner, 'this is Woody Hayes' daughter.' After a few minutes of consultation, he approached my window once again: 'Well, since you're guests in our city, what can we do to help?'

" 'We're lost, officer, and could use some assistance getting back to our hotel, the Huntington Sheraton.'

"After pausing to consider how to help, he took charge: 'Please follow us and we'll make sure you get home safely.'

"We fell in behind the cruiser and were escorted across L.A., right up to the front door of our hotel!"

"On one Rose Bowl trip, Coach Hayes quartered the Buckeyes at the Passionate Father's Monastery in the foothills outside Pasadena, bypassing the New Year's Eve revelry at our Huntington Sheraton headquarters," recalled Sandy.

"You can imagine how staying at a monastery went over with the players, souring their festive mood. It didn't bother Esco a bit, however, because a number of the good Fathers were South Benders. They broke out their favorite cognac and wine and stayed up half the night to talk football with Esco, especially about the Buckeyes and Fighting Irish.

"Among the favorite games they discussed was the '35 classic between Notre Dame and Ohio State in which the underdog Irish team pulled out a last-minute 18-15 upset in Ohio Stadium, and won a return engagement the next year by a score of 7-2.

"Esco was welcomed as the resident expert despite taunting his Irish hosts for no longer having the courage to schedule the Buckeyes."

One morning, prompted by the Buckeye's trip to the Rose Bowl in '98, I asked Sark: "Would you like to go to the Rose Bowl one more time?"

"I don't think so, Bill," he replied, "I've already been there nine times and there just wouldn't be much new in the experience...a major bowl game involves a lot of work. No, I'll be content to stay home and watch the game on TV."

Trivia

You will be remembered by what you leave behind. —*Old saying*

"Between academics and football, Buckeye players don't get much sleep," Coach began, "and my ends were lethargic at the start of the day. So, to get my players moving in the morning, I introduced a little fun with a daily trivia quiz, often inventing my own questions. The reward for a right answer was my own glass of orange juice. One question which usually stumped my players was: 'What three sports are won by going backwards?'

"The answers are:
- rowing (crew),
- backstroke in swimming, and
- tug-of-war.

"Rowing and backstroke usually came quickly. Tug-of-war took much much longer as a rule, perhaps several days or so."

"Tom Skladany and I got to talking about the trivia question on winning backwards," recalled Coach, "and I challenged him to solve it. He had all the correct answers in a day or two and was rather pleased with himself.

" 'That's real good,' I complimented Tom, 'but there is another answer out there that no one ever figured out. Why don't you try to come up with the fourth sports event that is won by going backwards?'

"Skladany set himself to the task, unsuccessfully. Every couple months or so, he would corner me and ask me to tell him the fourth event. I never did, but encouraged him to keep trying—to not give up. Months stretched into years and still there was no correct answer.

"Finally, Skladany sat down with me for a drink at the opening of the Buckeye Hall of Fame cafe (in 1997), and made one last appeal: 'Coach, I've been working on your trivia question for more than twenty years. Don't you think you could finally tell me what the fourth sporting event is?'

"And I answered: 'Gee, Tom, did I really say four?' "

I found it very easy to be drawn personally into Sark's trivia world, the result of talking with John Daly, a retired OSU tennis coach. After more than twenty years, Daly could still remember one of Sark's many questions:

"Can you name the three NFL teams whose names do not end with the letter S?"

Unfortunately, the former coach could not remember the answer—and I was challenged as were Sark's players decades ago.

I first began by listing the present NFL teams on a pad, but every one I could think of ended in S. Then I thought to check the Football Hall of Fame web site. To my chagrin—starting with the Arizona Cardinals and ending with the Washington Redskins—the names of all thirty-three present members of the NFL end in the letter S.

Then, I spent more hours on the web researching the histories of all present teams and scanned some library books on NFL history. Here is what I found out:

The four NFL team names not ending in S are:

Providence Steam Roller

Racine Legion

Card-Pitt

Phil-Pitt

The Phil-Pitt name was used in Philadelphia, and originated during a WW II player shortage when the Eagles combined with the Pittsburgh Steelers for one year. However, the team was called the Steagles in Pittsburgh, so I'm not sure that the Phil-Pitt moniker truly meets Esco's criterion. But the Card-Pitt name does, and was used during a brief period when the Chicago Cardinals and Pittsburgh were combined.

A week later, as Coach Daly and I were screening game films from Sark's All-American year, I mentioned the torturous effort required to identify the NFL team names not ending in S. It turns out that there was another, general version of Sark's trivia question:

"Can you name three professional football

teams whose names do not end with the letter S?"

The answers to this question are a lot easier, but still difficult, and is probably the version Sark used to stymie his ends at breakfast.

Answers from the World Football League are:

Chicago Fire (later the Chicago Wind)

Philadelphia Bell

Portland Storm (later the Portland Thunder)

Shreveport Steamer

Southern California Sun

Those from the United States Football League are the:

Chicago Blitz

Denver Gold

Los Angeles Express

As I was playing around with Coach's unanswered trivia questions, he must have been looking down over my shoulder, urging me to join his game by testing the wits of readers. Here are a couple of Sark spinoffs to consider:

1. Which is the only team to win an NFL championship with a name not ending in S?

Answer: The Providence Steamroller, in 1928.

2. Can you name four professional football teams that used the same names as professional baseball teams in the same city?

There are many answers:

Boston Braves

Louisville Colonels

Brooklyn Dodgers

New York Giants

Buffalo Bisons

New York Yankees

Cincinnati Reds

Pittsburgh Pirates

Cleveland Indians

St. Louis Cardinals

Detroit Tigers

Washington Senators

Use of the same team name was not always concurrent.

3. For hometown fans: name the four professional football teams that have represented Columbus, Ohio:

Answer: Columbus Panhandles, Bulls, Colts, and Caps.

The Panhandles date from the early days of

pro football. The Bulls were a late-thirties team. The Colts and Caps were the same team but played under different ownerships, according to Gene Fekete who coached both teams.

According to George Hill, Sark rated each stadium scouted on the basis of the quality of food served in the press box for the halftime buffet—a perk for visiting scouts and the journalists covering the game. The best? Sark rated Wisconsin number one on the strength of the cheeses, bratwurst, and sausages they served.

Vintage Sark

How many makes of car start with "P"?
None—they all start with gasoline!—Sark

Sark would take recruits to the Buckeye Grove and explain the tradition of planting a Buckeye tree for each OSU All-American. After finishing the story, he would ask the prospect: "Do you know how to pick out the Sarkkinen Tree?"

"No," was the usual reply, leaving Coach to explain:

"It's the one with the biggest nuts!"

"When I arrived at Ohio State in 1953," Bobby Watkins recalled, "Coach Sarkkinen greeted me with questions:

" 'What kind of player do you want to be?'

" 'I want to be a running back.'

" 'What kind of running back do you want to be?'

" 'I want to be a good running back.'

" 'Do you know what a good running back is?'

" 'No, I don't.'

" 'A good running back is a Big Ten Running Back.'

" 'What's that?'

" 'A Big Ten Running Back is not a Fancy Dan. He's big. He's strong. He breaks tackles. He runs over people. That's the kind of running back we want at Ohio State.'

"Right then," Watkins commented, "I decided what kind of running back I wanted to be."

Bobby Watkins did indeed become a Big Ten Running Back, one who was named to *Jet* magazine's All-America team and later played for the Chicago Bears.

"I was the first kicking specialist to receive a scholarship at Ohio State," said Tom Skladany, a three-time All-American, "but there was little satisfaction to be gained from this fact. The pressure to perform as a punter was intense right from the start when Coach Hayes informed me:

'You're the first punter I've ever given a scholarship, Skladany, and if you don't come through, I'm going to take it away from you!'

"The pressure from Coach Hayes was relentless. During fall practice, we usually wrapped up each day with five kicking plays. Woody invariably hovered over me on these kicking plays, about four or five yards off my shoulder.

"One afternoon, as we were preparing for the Minnesota game (1973), practice wound down in the usual way. My first four punts were beautiful bombs—high, long, perfect spirals. I didn't hit the fifth ball right and it tumbled end over end for about forty yards. Still not a bad punt, but Woody was not pleased, and reacted:

" 'If you can punt four great balls in a row, Skladany, you can sure kick five. How come you didn't punt the last ball like the first four? I want you to punt the fifth ball again, and if you don't get it right, I'm going to come right over there and kick you!'

"These gruff words unnerved me and I shanked my sixth punt badly, about thirty yards as I recall. True to his word, Woody stomped over and gave me a swipe on my backside with his foot. It didn't hurt, of course, but in the midst of my teammates, I was stunned with embarrassment.

"While still standing alone after everyone had left for the locker room, Sark walked up and asked: 'What's the matter, Tom?'

" 'Are you serious, Coach, you saw what happened.' But Sark interrupted.

" 'You don't understand, Tom. What happened was a terrific way to prepare for tomorrow's game.'

" 'How do you figure that, Coach?'

" 'It's easy: Coach Hayes just proved to you that you could kick four magnificent punts in a row under pressure from him and that's more than what you'll have to do in most of our games. Tomorrow, you'll probably have to punt about two or three times and you sure won't have to worry about Woody.'

" 'How come?'

" 'Think about it. Coach Hayes will be about forty yards away. You won't be able to see him because he'll be lost in the sideline crowd. You'll never be able to hear him because the crowd noise will be overwhelming. The pressure you've been under will be gone—and the kicking conditions will be absolutely perfect!"

"Sark was right. Practicing under pressure had prepared me for game situations and I was at ease the next afternoon. Even today, I still marvel at Sark's insight into the dynamics of Woody's coaching and how he used it to help me get ready for my first game."

"While at Ohio State," Coach recalled, "Les Horvath made All-American and won the Heisman Trophy. After graduation, he played for the Cleveland Rams and stayed with the team when it moved to Los Angeles. The charming stewardess on all of the team's charter flights, Shirley, in time became his wife. Les's new bride was not a knowledgeable football fan, as he quickly discovered.

"When they set up their household, Les proudly put his Heisman Trophy on the living room mantle, much to Shirley's chagrin. With tact, Les explained its unique tradition, especially important to himself. Shirley relented in the interest of marital harmony but nonetheless had her reservations about having a heavy chunk of cast bronze as the focal point of their home.

"One Saturday evening, Les and a bunch of his football pals arranged a progressive series of house parties. Departing the Horvath home, the party shifted to the home of Glenn Davis, the former Mr. Outside of Army's famous backfield. In an obvious place of honor stood another Heisman Trophy. Shirley locked on Les's eyes and slowly directed them to the Davis' Heisman with a look of skepticism.

"During the course of the party, Doc Blanchard, the former Mr. Inside of Army's backfield, arrived and also was introduced as a Heisman recipient. Now there were three trophy winners in the crowd, further deflating the significance of the Heisman, at least in Shirley's estimation.

"Later in the evening, the party shifted to Tom Harmon's home and, sure enough, there was another Heisman Trophy on conspicuous display. With her skepticism at its peak, Shirley arched her eyebrows and said to Les:

"It appears to me that everyone playing college football has a Heisman Trophy!"

"I don't know what the odds are of partying with four Heisman Trophy winners in the course of one night, but they've got to be pretty high," Coach concluded with obvious merriment.

"At the start of the 1973 season, I promised to treat my graduate assistants to dinner in San Francisco, if Ohio State won the Rose Bowl," recalled George Hill, defensive coordinator for Ohio State and the Miami Dolphins. "When we won, I asked Esco for suggestions on where to take them. Esco knew all the best restaurants in every city in the country. He recommended Ernie's. 'It's a real nice place for dinner,' he said.

"Grateful for the suggestion, I invitedSark to join us. Esco had picked exceedingly well—I all but choked when the tab for five all-star meals was presented. Esco, unconcerned, enjoyed his meal immensely."

Self-Portrait

This above all: to thine own self be true.
—William Shakespeare

How would you describe yourself? Would you write a memoir? Compose an essay? Write a paragraph? Whatever the chosen means, the task is a difficult one. In several personal notes written in the later years of his life, Coach sketched a portrait of himself in "the words that describe me best:" These six words are: Laconic — Phlegmatic — Stoic — Patronizing — Analytical — and Ingratiating.

This crisp portrait is unusual from several standpoints: all of the words are rather uncommon and some of their meanings are negative in terms of common usage today.

As Coach obviously spent some time selecting these precise words, I consulted a *Random House Collegiate Dictionary* and *Webster's College Thesaurus* to learn more about them. The following definitions are a blend of these two sources:

Laconic: Using few words; concise, brief, succinct, pithy; concentrated, to the point.

Phlegmatic: Not easily excited to action or display of emotion, calm, serene, self-possessed; cool.

Stoic: Free from passion, unmoved by joy and grief; detached; philosophic; acceptance of unavoidable necessity.

Patronizing: Encouragement or support of an institution or enterprise; support as a patron; to give one's patronage.

Analytical: Skilled in or habitually using analysis, i.e., the separating of any material or abstract quality into its constituent parts; a method of studying the nature of something or determining its essential features and their relationships.

Ingratiating: Charming, agreeable, pleasing; meant to gain favor; to establish oneself in the favor or good graces of another.

In these few words, there is an amazing agreement between how Sark viewed himself and how colleagues, friends, and family members perceived him. His insight into himself was as keen and sharp as his insights into others.

Esco in retirement

Family & Friends

God sees the truth, but waits.—Proverb

Few people are aware of the family difficulties faced by Esco and Freda Sarkkinen. A private person, Coach mentioned the tragic circumstances brought to my attention by his daughter, Sandy.

"While Esco was still in the Coast Guard, my brother, Kim, was born in 1945 with an immune system deficiency, requiring a sterile environment to sustain life. The cause of the deficiency was a recessive gene carried by both of my parents—a once in a million occurrence, according to physicians. During the year Kim lived, because of the demands placed on my parents, I resided with my grandmother on the family farm near Portsmouth, Ohio.

"With astronomical odds against a repeat occurrence, my parents were told it would be okay to have another child. My sister, Karina, was born in 1948, a couple of years after Esco joined the OSU coaching staff. Against all odds, Karina had the same immune deficiency as Kim, requiring the same sterile isolation. She lived about one year while I once again went to live on the family farm. So, in their early years together, Esco and Freda had to contend with heart-rending stress and losses. My parents considered adoption but decided to stick it out with just me.

"Our family life started to revolve around Esco's coaching career, which Freda supported wholeheartedly. I became a Buckeye brat who went to University School and later worked part-time in the Athletic Office. I often had lunch with Esco and rode back and forth to school with him and my mother. Buckeye players and staff in a way became my extended family.

"I believe Esco was very satisfied and content to be an assistant coach because it provided him the opportunity of working closely with young men every day. The longevity Woody Hayes brought to the OSU program fit well with the stable lifestyle my parents seemed to need and enjoy. To have opted for the many uncertainties of new coaching opportunities, usually short-term and risky, would have meant relinquishing much that my parents had accomplished under trying circumstances.

"Moreover, for all his laid-back and jovial demeanor, Esco was first and foremost a committed football coach. He was intensely dedicated to winning and was willing to put forth the effort necessary. The exceptional talents of coaches and players at Ohio State allowed him to realize this deep, dominating desire while meeting other needs.

"I am often asked to explain the lengthy, close

Esco remained a faithful OSU fan

coaching relationship between Woody Hayes and Esco. The question comes to mind because the emotionally-involved, hard-charging Woody Hayes was a sharp contrast to the reserved, unflappable personal bearing of my father.

"Woody and Esco each held each other in high professional regard and were friendly toward each other—the kind of closeness which develops with the pursuit of shared purpose, values, and commitments. This kind of friendship transcended the usual kind of social friendships most people revere, and it is fair to note that Woody and Esco moved in different social circles. They were certainly cordial toward one another, but between them conventional social considerations were secondary. What really kept Woody and Esco together, I believe, was their love of the game and their desire to play it at the highest level— and Ohio State gave them both this opportunity."

"Esco was right at home in the ethnic diversity found in Cleveland and northeastern Ohio,"

said Sandy on another occasion. "He loved recruiting there and enjoyed relationships with many players from this region because of his own immigrant background.

"Esco's parents had immigrated from Finland as a couple. Earlier, his father, when seeking a mate, had traveled from Finland to Russia to 'find a wife from good solid stock,' one who was fun to be around. By his choice of a Russian wife, humor was introduced into our family.

"When I was young, for instance, my Finnish-Russian grandmother persuaded me to believe that she was the lost princess, Anastasia. At our tea parties, she encouraged me to crook my little finger when holding a cup—'like royalty.' She persisted in this Russian royalty scam throughout my childhood years.

"Finnish was the language used in the home and Esco could speak it fluently. This language skill 'purchased' him a couple of trips to his family home and major cities in Finland when he was occasionally asked to accompany U.S. sports teams as an interpreter and guide.

"When he was young, Esco played soccer and

ran track, the favored sports in his European-like community. As he grew up, he became actively involved in basketball and American football. The first football game his father ever saw was when Esco played in high school.

"Esco loved recruiting in northeastern Ohio because he could sit and tarry with immigrant parents from Finland, Russia, Poland, Hungary and other European countries. Recruiting often occurred over ethnic meals and desserts which delighted his palette. He was a hit with mothers, and when their sons came to play at Ohio State, he was assured of a steady stream of plates and trays full of tasty ethnic delicacies."

Said Greg Lashutka, "Esco Sarkkinen was quite a cook and gourmet. Whenever I ran across an interesting dish in a magazine, or had a particularly fine entreé while traveling or dining out, I would get the recipe and send it to Sark."

"I enjoyed a close personal relationship with Coach Sarkkinen for many years," said Tom Marendt who played under him for several years.

"As Esco had all the qualifications necessary to direct a major football program, I was always curious as to why he didn't pursue a head coaching career. Occasionally I would ask: How come you didn't go on to head coaching?

"Most of the time, Esco's responses were vague or unrevealing. On one occasion, however, he gave me an answer I feel came close to the truth:

" 'If I had become a head coach, Tom, I would have had to remain aloof from my players.'

"Whether or not this was the complete answer I don't know, because Coach never expounded upon it. The way he treated his players, however, leads me believe that day-to-day, close working relationships with young men were exceedingly important to him. As in my case, many of his on-field associations grew into life-long friendships."

Coach could keep a ruse alive for many decades, no matter how improbable. One of these began in collusion with his younger brother, Eino, when they were both students at Ohio State:

The Sarkkinen brothers were often photographed and written up as a duo. On one occasion, when they met with a cub reporter for yet another sports story of this ilk, the interview developed along typical lines. It was replete with inane platitudes about family, brother, team, and coaches—pretty smaltzy stuff.

However, as the interview was about to conclude, Esco surprised the inexperienced scribe with a family revelation: "No article on the Sarkkinen brothers would be complete," he said, "without a few paragraphs on our younger brother, Elmo." Brother Elmo, both brothers confided, was the stellar star of their gridiron family. In fact, Elmo was good enough to make Buckeye fans forget Esco and Eino had ever played at Ohio State. But, there was a problem: "Elmo has already decided to play for Southern California!"

The interview revealing brother Elmo and his defection ran unchecked in the press, and after the story broke, the roof caved in. Irate Buckeye fans began calling the athletic office to complain about the loss of a promising Buckeye standout to the Trojans, particularly galling because of Elmo's family ties to Ohio State. Recruiting oversight and ineptness were voiced.

All of this was puzzling to members of the coaching staff because none of them could ever recall having met or heard about brother Elmo. When the coaching staff got to checking facts, though, they finally discovered that Elmo was a fictional character—and had a few choice words for the editor who had run the unverified story.

But brother Elmo would not die an ignoble death on the editorial floor. Sark continued to speak of him as if he was a real live person—and sixty years later, brother Elmo still enjoys permanent status within the Sarkkinen family. He often "attends" family functions and is spoken of in the present tense; folks are "sorry" about the times when he can't show up.

Even outside the family, you can still hear an occasional reference to Coach's brother Elmo.

Six decades after Elmo made his debut in print,

I found myself taking the bait at Coach's funeral service, where I met his family for the first time. Sandy, his daughter, was kind enough to briefly introduce me to other family members. Pointing toward Esco's real brother, standing across the room, she said: "Besides talking with Eino, you should be sure to talk with Esco's brother, Elmo— he was standing beside Eino just a few minutes ago but seems to have wandered off. I can't help you find him at the moment but you shouldn't have any trouble finding him. Just ask around— everyone knows brother Elmo."

Even though I thought it odd that Coach had never mentioned his brother, Elmo, I cased the funeral home thoroughly in an effort to meet and talk with him. Finally, about an hour later, I learned the truth—brother Elmo was a figment of Esco's imagination!

After a family gathering for Father's Day in 1992, Esco and Freda returned home. Tired from the day's activities, Esco turned in early. Freda stayed up to watch the late movies in their television room, as was her custom. In the morning, Esco peeked in, but thought she was still sleeping. On closer inspection, however, he found she had suffered a heart attack and died in her sleep.

During the last six years of his life, Esco lived alone in their modest brick home near campus—well, almost alone. He was tended to by a live-in companion, Norman—a silky, coal-black cat. Norman became a close companion—Sark frequently signed his correspondence "Esco and Norman Sark-kinen." As friends discovered who Norman was, they joined in the pretense, addressing their letters to Esco in the same way.

Norman on Esco's senior letter blanket

Reflections

Choose an occupation that you like and you may never have to work a day in your life.
                    —Confucius

Coach was seventy-six years old when we became acquainted. He was stocky with squared-off shoulders and in good shape for his age. His eyes were always bright, twinkling behind heavy glasses. Most of the time, he wore gray slacks, a scarlet or gray sweater, a scarlet windbreaker, and a classic Block O coach's cap—black like Woody's. Still projecting granite strength and determination, I could easily visualize Coach rolling up the cuffs of his pants and taking to the field once again.

Esco had the strong, massive hands of a football lineman, easily bearing the huge gold rings that he wore. On one hand was a Big Ten Championship ring and on the other was a National Championship ring—bolstering his physical presence. One morning, I asked him: "How many gold rings do you have, Coach?"

"Lets see," he said, "I have a lot more rings than I have fingers to wear them on...five National Championship rings and thirteen Big Ten Championships rings...that makes a total of eighteen gold rings."

Quite a haul! This record of achievement is made even more remarkable by the seventeen gold charms (miniature football pants) awarded to him for victories over Michigan. These coveted symbols Coach modestly fashioned into a charm bracelet for his wife, Freda, which she wore to Buckeye games for good luck.

What strikes me now—several years later—is

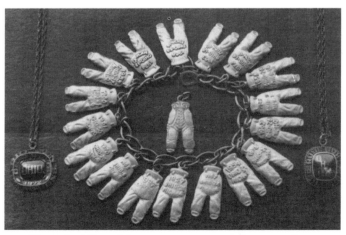

Esco's 17 gold pants, two pendants, plus
a gold pants inscribed "WH"—for Woody Hayes

that Coach never expounded upon the personal aspects of his playing and coaching achievements. For instance, upon hearing that Esco was an All-American, I asked him about it.

His reply was brief: "Yes, I made All-American when I was a senior, in 1939." And that was all—nothing about the games he played, the passes he caught, the blocks and tackles he made, the high points or low. He must have been an extraordinary player because the famous All-American back, Tom Harmon, in a radio interview, said Sark was the "toughest opponent" he had ever played.

Indeed, in order to write this tribute to Coach, I have had to learn a lot about the man who had befriended me in the simplest of ways—in conversation over morning coffee. It is evident to me now that the old professor was still in action, making me do the work of learning about him and the Buckeyes.

As I was putting the finishing touches on this text, a cache of old football game films was found in a locked storeroom in Ohio Stadium. I happened to see one of these films broadcast on television. It pictured the transition from one era to another—the Buckeyes were running the split-T formation while their opponents stuck to the single-wing. I immediately realized that Coach's 36-year playing-coaching career had spanned several great eras of Ohio State football.

The first era was the running, punting power game of the first half of the 1900's that Coach experienced as a player; the second was post-war quarter-century when deception and finesse were integrated with the historic power game, and the passing attack gained in importance, occuring while Esco served as an assistant coach.

In retirement, Coach lived to witness another quarter-century of dramatic change in college football due to social shifts, scholarship rule changes, professional intrusiveness, administrative and financial restructuring, and television exposure.

By sharing his over-arching experience, Coach slowly and subtlety introduced me to college football as it is played at the highest level. As a result, my esteem for players and coaches grew without my being aware of it. A greater sense of empathy and respect for their dedication, discipline, and values evolved, and the word TRADITION took on new meaning. In short, Sark had enriched my life!

A few weeks after I finished this collection of anecdotes, I was powerfully reminded that Sark had enriched the lives of just about everyone he met. I met Coach George Hill at an afternoon gathering. He described Sark's method of speaking up during coach roundtables.

"Sark would sit quietly while he listened to all of us young turks make our suggestions. Then someone would ask him what he thought. He would respond by saying, 'Well, we tried that in 1953, and these were the problems we ran into.'

"In this nonjudgmental way, Sark led us younger coaches to probe and reassess our own thinking. I learned a lot in this simple way.'

"Sark was a genius when it came to coaching."

The Victory Bell

Allahu Akbar! Arabic for 'God is great!'
                              —*Esco Sarkkinen*

On Saturday, February 28, 1998 in Columbus, Ohio, Coach Esco Sarkkinen passed away at the age of seventy-nine. His funeral service was the most unusual one I have ever attended—one where joy and good humor prevailed over loss and sadness. After the service and eulogies, Mill Street Bagels catered a family luncheon which featured his favorite sandwich—vegetable fixin's on a vegan bagel, grey poupon mustard, no mayo.

The following morning, a solemn funeral procession toured the main campus, slowly skirting the practice fields and stadium where Coach had given his active life to the Scarlet and Gray. As his long entourage inched past Ohio Stadium, I could "hear" the Victory Bell, silently tolling.

ESCO SARKKINEN
1918-1998
An Ohio State Man

Acknowledgements

Special thanks go to former Buckeye coaches and players for granting interviews for this book.

I am deeply endebted to Sandra Sue Sarkkinen Hayes for family history and photographs. Assistance has also come from David Hayes and Stephanie Stewart at the University of Colorado; Toim Mattingly at the University of Tennessee; Ron Biddle; Paul Gelacek; Douglas Goodsell; Jean Gordon; Gene Fekete; Robert G. Smoth; Pandel Savic; James DeLeone; Mildred Sarkkinen; and friends at Mill Street Bagels.

Appreciation also goes to: John Daly and Mark Smith at the OSU Athletic Department Archives; Jana Drvota and Berta Ihnat at the Ohio State University Archives; Susan Ferguson of the Varsity O Alumni Association; the OSU Athletic Communications Office; and the Buckeye Sports Bulletin.

I also wish to express wholehearted gratitude to Carl Japikse, my editor, and Ann, my wife, both of whom have marvelously supported *An Ohio State Man* from its inception.

Permissions & Credits

Permissions

Judge Steven B. Hayes has given permission for use of material written and copyrighted by Wayne Woodrow Hayes. Photographs and materials from the OSU archives and athletic department are used by permission.

Photo Credits

Ron Biddle—cover photo and page 12; OSU Archives—pages 6, 23, and 52; OSU Athletic Department Archives—page 2; Columbus Citizen—page 27; Sarkkinen family scrapbook—pages 1, 17, 25, 30, 68, 79, 90, 117, 139, 141, 150, and 157; Chance Brockway—pages 19, 35, 102, and 152; Pandel Savic—page 86; andUniversity of Colorado Sports Information—page 98.

The Point After

Additional copies of *An Ohio State Man* can be purchased at local bookstores, or directly from the publisher, Enthea Press.

To order from the publisher, the cost is $14.99 per copy plus $4 for shipping. Send a check or money order for the correct amount to Enthea Press, P.O. Box 297, Marble Hill, GA 30148. In Georgia, please add 7 percent sales tax.

Orders can also be placed by telephone, fax, or e-mail and charged to MasterCard, VISA, American Express, Diners, or Discover. To order by telephone, please call 1-800-336-7769 from 10 to 5 p.m. Monday or Wednesday, or from 9 to 1 p.m. on Thursday. Send faxes to 1 - (706) 579-1865. To order by internet, send an e-mail to: entheapress@worldnet.att.net.

Multiple copies of the book can be ordered at discounted prices: 10 or more copies cost $12 a copy, plus $8 for shipping; 25 or more copies cost $10 a copy, plus $12 for shipping.